TREASURES
~ IN ~
PRAYER

TREASURES
~ IN ~
PRAYER

JONATHAN OGOGO

BALBOA.
PRESS
A DIVISION OF HAY HOUSE

Balboa Press books may be ordered through booksellers or by contacting:

Balboa Press
A Division of Hay House
1663 Liberty Drive
Bloomington, IN 47403
www.balboapress.com
1 (877) 407-4847

Scripture taken from the King James Version of the Bible.

Printed in the United States of America.

ISBN: 978-1-5043-2519-6 (e)
ISBN: 978-1-5043-2518-9 (sc)

Balboa Press rev. date: 2/11/2015

CONTENTS

INTRODUCTION

People need to be taught from the bible how to pray as a truly as they need to be taught how to preach or win souls. John the Baptist taught his disciples how to pray and same, the twelve disciples came to him saying "Lord teaches us how to pray, as John taught his disciples". Even Ethiopian eunuch who was asked by Philip, do you understands thou that readiest? And he replied. How can I; except someone should guide me?

The modernists have shows, there is a deep hunger of heart to learn to pray aright and get things from God. If I can, bridge the gap this hunger of the people of God and to help men, women and young people really to pray, to ask and receive, is my purpose in writing this book.

Based on what prayer real is, "we have not because we ask not" individuals, the churches are powerless. Christians are neither happy nor prosperous in spiritual matters, our loved ones are unsaved, all because we do not effectually, spiritually, gets hold of God in prayer. When we remedy the prayer life of the people of God, we remedy what is wrong with Christians and churches and open the way for every needed blessing. What this book set out to do is to teach people how to pray according to the scripture and to stimulate faith in God who answers prayer. The bible gives many great and exceedingly precious promises about what God will do for those who come to him in prayer and the bible clearly gives the conditions for getting things from God.

The condition is that you must ask. "Ask and it shall be given to you (Matt. 7:7) "Ask and you shall receive (John 16:24) that is prayer, prayer is asking and an answer to prayer is receiving.

I have tried and proved, as matter of personal testimony. I know that God answers prayers. He has answered mine in many ways, so clearly out of the realm of probability that is unbiased investigator must be convinced that these answers to prayer were really the supernatural intervention of a loving God who works miracles for his children when they trust him. Others ought to tell what God has done for them and I ought to tell what God has done for me too.

To God be the Glory, My wife and I prayed for accommodation problem when we wanted to relocate, we did not even have the money for it but God answered our prayer through my in-law who was in abroad for unexpected dollars sent to us via his junior brother? The money has been with his brother for 2 months while the brother has been searching for our address. Even many other instances where the fund for my education was difficult to raise, God answers the prayer and see me through the crucibles.

And, humbly, I dare hope that God will make the book a blessing to hundreds as it teaches people to pray according to bible, urges them to pray more and gives remarkable incidents of answered prayer.

I shall feel wonderfully repaid, if whenever people read this book, they will really turn to God in believing, persistent, importunate, surrendered, unceasing, expectant prayer to God.

With a confession of my own weakness, with an earnest exhortation to others that we really come back to the bible teaching and to bible examples of prayer and with a fervent hope that God may use this book to the blessing of hundreds, I commit it to God.

As for me, I love the Lord, because he hath heard my voice and my supplications. Because he hath induced his ear unto me, will I call upon him as long as I live? Therefore I will call upon thou Lord, he is great to be praise, thou Lord is right.

CHAPTER ONE

GOD THAT ANSWERS' PRAYER

Our God is a God who hears and answers prayer. Prayer hearing is one of His attributes of God and a part of his nature. Praying first in everything you do gives him power to hear your prayer as palmist put it. "Thou that hearest prayer" (Psalm 65:2). In everything we do we should hand it over to him by asking through prayer. Prayer is asking. God holiness and his righteousness never vary. He is always holy, always righteous, his characteristics and attributes of God are unchanging and everlasting. He says, "I am the Lord, I change not" (Mal. 3:6) "Jesus Christ the same Yesterday and today and forever" (Heb. 13:8) God is in all generations the same God who delights to hear and does hear and answer's prayer, when we present our case to him first in every endeavors in our life.

If there are ever conditions that hinder prayer, the conditions are on the part of the one who prays and not on God's part. It is a part of his nature, as his mercy, his justice, his righteousness, his omnipotence. "O thou that hearest prayer, unto thee shall all flesh come".

Prayer is almost universal in mankind, unsaved men pray. All nations pray. It is the same of need, of weakness, that leads men to cry out of help to a higher power and it is wrong to say, as some have said, that the prayers of unconverted people are never heard.

Before anyone can come to God, he must believe two things.

First – He must believe that there is a God.

Second – He must believe that God is a rewarder of them that diligently seek him. All other things implied and understood, if you know that much about our infinite blessing, merciful, prayer hearing and prayer answering God.

It becomes clear, to them that when we limit God's willingness to answer prayer, we are guilty of a horrible sin of unbelief. To limit God in his willingness to hear and answer prayer for those who diligently seek him is belief in the very nature of God himself. We ought rather to put limitation on men and frankly confess that we have not because we ask not, that we ask --- that we might consume it on our lusts (James 4:2-3) God always saved people by faith in church and no other way God has always been holy, always has been almighty, always has been merciful and so God has always been the God who hears and answers prayer. Even God made the animals, makes food for them; he made plant, causes the rain to fall and the sun to shine upon them. The God who made the honeybee made flower for nectar. For every living thing there is a place of food, a protection, a provision from the hand of an infinite God. Don't these things show that there is a want, a need, a desire, God wants to fill it, where there is a hunger, and God wants to satisfy it?

Prayer becomes the most compelling Christian duty on earth. God never commended us to sing without ceasing, nor preach without ceasing, nor give without ceasing nor work without ceasing but he did commend "pray without ceasing" (1 Thess. 5:17). After Solomon Built the temple at Jerusalem and dedicated it to the God – God did say, "Now, mine eyes shall be open and mine ears attend unto the prayer that is made in this place" (2 Chron. 7:15) God did say in Isaiah 56:7 "For mine house shall be called a house of prayer for all people". The temple was house of prayer for all people, backed all the preaching the prayer, the prophesying the prayer, the singing the prayer, back all religions observances, God intended there should be a living faith – in a God who hears and answers prayer. There is nothing pleasing God without prayer.

THE FACT ABOUT GOD

When one understands that God hears and answers prayer, then his faculty perceives all the attributes, all the nature of God. All the other qualities or attributes or characteristics of God are implied when we understand that He answers prayer.

First – A prayer – hearing God is a living God. He is not an idol of wood, or stone or house object. The priest of Baal on Mount Carnal cried out to their god. "O Baal hear us" There was none who neither answered nor regarded them (1 Kings 18:26) Baal has eyes but sees not, it has mouth, but speaks not, it has ears but it hears not because it is not a living idol but our God is a living God that Hearst prayer.

Secondly, a prayer – hearing and answering God is an all-knowing God an omniscient. Does God hear and answer the cry of millions of His people in all the nations at the same time and languages? Does he sees the faith, supplications and sincerity or perceive the hearts of those who pray? God knows all things, He is a limitless God.

Thirdly – If God is able to answer prayer, then He has all power in heaven and on earth. If God can answer prayer for rain, He control it weather, crops, sun, insects, moisture and even the germ of life in the seed itself. If God answered the prayer of Joshua so that the sun stood still in its relation to the earth for about the space of a day (Joshua 10:12, 13) then our God controls the whole infinite universe.

Fourthly – If God answers prayer, such almighty power, there could be none other as powerful as and none to dispute his right, even in the very nature of the case, He is the creator of the Heaven and Earth.

Fifty – The God who answers prayer is a miracle – working God, Believe that God is a rewarder of them that diligently seek him means that one has faith in all that is ever claimed for God.

DOES GOD WORK MIRACLES TODAY'S LIFE?

Someone may ask. The answer is capital YES, and then His ordinary and natural way of working in answering prayer would be by miracles.

Every soul saved is a supernatural act, not a natural one. Every time God intervenes and controls nature or changes a plan to make it divine favor when it otherwise would not have favored, it is someone's prayed, then that is a miracle. A God who would cease to work miracles would cease to be a God in the bible sense, that is, a personal God who personally hears and answers the prayer of faith.

Sixthly – If God answers prayer, then he is a God of infinite love and mercy. God loves sinners, his mercy is boundless. "Where sin abounded, grace did much more abound" (Rom. 5:20).

When one really believes that God is a prayer hearing and answering God, he has the secret to the very heart of God, and he can divinely see and outline all the graces and powers and majesty on the infinite God.

WONDERFUL WORK OF GOD

All nature speaks of a wonderful works of God, a God who made man, who loves him, and who wants to provide all his needs. Psalm 65: 9-13 says "Thou visited the earth and wateriest it, thou greatly enrich it with the river of God, which is full of water, thou prepare them corn, when thou hast so provided for it. Thou wateriest the ridges thereof abundantly, thou settles the furrows thereof, thou makes it soft with showers, thou blesses the springing thereof, thou crownest the year with thy goodness, and thy paths drop fatness. They drop upon the pastures of the wilderness, and the little hills rejoice on every side. The pastures are clothed with flocks, the valleys also are covered over with corn, they shout for joy, they also sing"

The psalmist, speaking by the Holy Spirit, seams to say that the God who loves to answer man's prayer has anticipated so many of his needs, has watered the ground that was dry, has given to the hungry flocks the pasture and has covered the valleys with corn for man and beast and these pastures and valleys shout for joy, and sing of the relevant, loving mercy of God. God even cares for the animals, In Psalm 104:15 says "Thou causeth the grass to grow for the cattle and herb for the service of man, that he may bring forth food out of the earth, and wine that maketh glad the heart of man and oil to make his face to shine and bread which strengthened man's heart".

Verse 18 continued "The high hills are a refuse for the wild goats and the rocks for the conies" while in verse 21 says "The young lions roar after their prey and seek their meat from God". And then also, the beasts and even of the sea, we were told that thou mayest give them their meat in due season that thou givest them they gather, thou openest thine hand, they are filled with good", the earth proves that God loves man, longs to bless him, longs to provide every need of mankind.

If God did not love man, life would have been extremingly impossible on this earth, if it had not been tailored exactly to fit man's needs. God made it just the right size. Or if three –fourths of the earth's surface were covered by land instead of by water, then the earth would simply be a giant desert, with fringes of vegetation around the seas, and the variation of temperatures would be so great it would be impossible for mankind to live. That is the wonderful name of our wonderful Lord as God reveals Himself in act.

CHAPTER TWO

THE REASONS FOR PRAYER

There are many reasons why we pray but the followings are God promises concerning the prayer and form the reasons, we adduce prayer.

1. That God insistently commends it in the bible.
2. That prayer is God's appointed way for Christians to get things.
3. That prayer is God's way of Christians to have fullness of Joy
4. That prayer is the way out of all trouble, the cure for all worry and anxious care.
5. That answered prayer is the only unanswerable argument against skepticism, unbelief, modernism and infidelity.
6. That whosoever shall call upon the name of the Lord shall be saved.
7. That prayer is the only way to have the power of the Holy Spirit for God's work.

We have out lined the most and seven (7) compelling reasons why people should pray and why everybody ought to pray, why prayer should be the most regular and continually thing in our lives.

It is an impelling duty which Jesus taught. "And he speaks a parable unto them to this end that men ought always to pray and not to faint"

(Luke 18:1). This parable was not that some men should pray, but that men, mankind everywhere and in all times should pray. Again he commanded men to pray without ceasing (1 Thess. 5:17) not only to pray but pray all time. Prayer should be continually turning of our hearts to God about everything we need and everything we want until our mind touch with God. As the case of mother in her sleep, listens for the cry of her baby, so a Christian's heart can be attuned to God while he is absorbed in daily duties or even when he sleep. A Christian should pray about everything. "Be careful for nothing but in everything by prayer and supplication with thanksgiving let your requests be made known unto God"'. (Philippians 4:6). Jesus commanded the apostles in (Matt. 28:20), then we, too, are to watch and pray lest we enter into temptation. Lack of prayer is sin. Samuel says to the people of Israel "God forbid that I should sin against the Lord in ceasing to pray for you". (1 Sam. 12:23).

PRAYER IS GOD'S APPOINTED WAY FOR CHRISTIAN TO GET THINGS.

God's children are taught that they are to get things by asking and that the reason we do not have is because we do not ask (James 4:2) "Ye have not because ye ask not, "fighting, warring, struggling and scheming are not God's way for Christians to get things. For you to get things you must ask God for it. The savior taught us to pray, "Give us this day our daily bread". (Matt. 6:11) The way to get daily bread is to ask God for it. The point I am making here is that whether God uses well –known means or does it by ways latterly unexpected or even by ways impossible with men, to answer your prayer, still it is God who gives what we need, we need to ask for it, praying is God's appointed way for a Christian to have what he needs and wants. Every other way may fail but God will never fail. Our father has appointed that his Children get things by prayer." Ye have not because ye ask not".

PRAYER IS GOD'S WAY FOR CHRISTIANS TO RECEIVE FULLNESS OF JOY

Christians ought to have their needs satisfied. Christians ought not to live defeated, unhappy lives, tormented by needs which cannot be met. So God has appointed the Christians to have fullness of joy all the time by having their prayers answered.

Imagine a young wife, married to a rich husband who so loves her and delights in her that he gives her everything for which she expresses a desire. Her life is filled with happiness because her husband loves her so much and gives her all the things for which her heart desires. That is what God does to his children. God can teach his children and lead them by the Holy Spirit to pray for the things that will bring fullness of joy and no course. "The blessing of the Lord maketh rich and he added no sorrow in it". (Provb. 10:22).

Prayer is the secret of constant joy, the secret really of "Fullness of Joy" Rich and full life of a Christian depends squarely on how much and how he prays. If you get on such praying ground that you can get things from God, get all the desires of your heart, get all that you need, then day to day you can live a victorious, happy life. Prayer is the secret of fullness of joy and for that reason Christians should pray.

PRAYER IS THE WAY OUT OF ALL TROUBLE, THE CURE FOR ALL WORRY AND ANXIOUS CARE.

Prayer is to make way to get rid of what you do not want and get out of trouble and away from worry and care. Philippians 4:6, 7 says "Be careful for nothing, but in everything by prayer and supplication with thanksgiving let your requests be made known unto God."

May the peace of God, which passeth all understanding, shall keep your hearts and minds through Christ Jesus. Amen.

God promises to those who bring everything to him in prayer with supplication and thanksgiving "the peace of God" which passeth all understanding shall Keep your hearts and minds through Christ Jesus. "Cashing all your care upon him, for he careth for you" (1 Peter 5:7) and casting thy burden upon the lord and he shall sustain thee" (Psalm 55:22) Every Christian ought to be marked by a calm, unworried frame of mind, a deep settled peace of heart that the world can never attain or give. One of the marks of a really successful happy Christian whose cares are all lay on the Lord Jesus. Every Christian ought to be able to boast in the Lord, as David did in (Psalm 34:6). "This poor man cried and the Lord heard him and saved him out of all his troubles". A Christian can take his burdens to the Lord and leave them there and have perfect peace. A Christian can make such a habit of praying about every need, every burden, every fret, every care, every problem until he can obey the command of savior to "take no thought for your life, what ye shall eat, or what ye shall drink, nor yet for your body, what ye shall put on" (Matt. 6:25). Prayer is the way out of trouble, the way to do away with worries and anxious care. Therefore, brethren, let us pray, even unceasingly.

ANSWERED PRAYER IS THE ONLY UNANSWERABLE ARGUMENT ON MODERNISM AND INFIDELITY

Without faith it is impossible to please God. Faith may be regarded as "for he that cometh to God must believe that he is and that he is a rewarder of them that diligently seek him. How can we convince those who do not believe there is God? Argument is sometimes necessary. The bible proves itself in the word of God. "All nature declares there is God, even the Heavens declare the glory of God and the firmament sheweth his handy work" (Psalm 19:1).

Elijah at mount carnal, gathered the people of Israel together to prove to them that the Lord was the true God and that the Idol Baal was not a god who could see or hear or help. When the four hundred and fifty prophets of Baal cried aloud in vain to their god and he could not answer by fire from Heaven, Elijah built an alter laid thereon the wood and the bullock put on fire under and poured over it twelve barrels of water, then he prayed that God would send fire from Heaven in the sight of all the people to burn up the sacrifice and prove that he is God. Elijah's prayer was "Lord God of Abraham, Isaac and Israel, let it be known this day that thou art God in Israel and that I am thy Servant and that I have done all these things at thy word. Hear me O' Lord, hear me, that these people may know that thou art the Lord of God and that thou has turned their heart back again". (1 Kings 18:36-37) And the answer came immediately, then the fire of the Lord fell and consumed the burned sacrifice and wood and the stones and the dust and licked up the water that was in the trench" (1 Kings 18:38). We ought to pray because God's answer to prayer is proof that can be put to rout all modernism and unbelief.

PRAYER IS THE ONLY WAY TO HAVE THE POWER OF HOLY SPIRIT FOR GOD'S WORK

It is unthinkable, foolish and wicked to try to do God's work without God's power (Moody. A.L in John R. RICE 1970). There is no way for a Christian to have God's power except by prayer. This is a plain promise in Luke 11:13 "If ye, being evil, know how to give good gifts unto your children, how much more shall your heavenly father give the Holy spirit to them that ask him". "God promised a blessed revival" "My people which are called by my name, shall humble themselves and pray and seek my face and turn from their wicked ways". (11 Chronicle 7:14). So the secret of power on preaching is in prayer. If any Christian longs to have a personal definite endowment of power, the power of the Holy Spirit, then, this is the way to have it, seek God's face in prayer with whatever confession and self – judgment and heart-surrender necessary as you wait on God, until the spirit of God can fill you and use you. The heart-broken, sin- confessing, penitent prayer was the secret of power every time the saints of God has seasons of revivals and every time individuals were filled with the spirit of God for blessed service.

WHOSOEVER SHALL CALL UPON THE NAME OF THE LORD SHALL BE SAVED

In Luke chapter 18: We see the poor republican who crying out "God be merciful to me a sinner", we see him going down to this house, justified, and saved that everyday. Another example is the dying thief who turned to Jesus, on the cross beside him and said, "Lord, remember me when thou comest into thy kingdom". And we hear the promise of the savior beside him. "To day shall thou be with me in Paradise" (Luke 23:39-43). So lost sinners have a right to pray and anyone who genuinely calls on the Lord for salvation will be saved. And deciding factor for salvation is the heart fainth.

"Believe in the Lord Jesus Christ and thou shall be saved". Again Jesus said "very, very. I say unto you, he that believeth in me hath ever lasting life" (John 6:47). Faith is a turning in his heart to depend on Christ. And God hears the faintest cry of the heart, without a whisper of breath, without a moving of the lips.

So, brethren, feel perfectly free to call on God for mercy and forgiveness and be assured that God will hear, that he does hear, that he has heard already when you call on him for forgiveness and salvation.

CHAPTER THREE

ASKING SOMETHING FROM GOD

Prayer is asking. God reacted many places in the bible, what he expect from us about asking.

1. Jesus says "Ask and it shall be given to you Matt. 7:7.
2. Jesus says "for everyone that asketh received" Matt. 7:8.
3. Jesus says "And all things, whatsoever ye shall ask in prayer, believing, ye shall receive' Matt. 21:22.
4. Jesus says" How much more shall your father who is in Heaven give goods things to them that ask him" Matt. 7:11
5. Jesus says "How much more shall your Heaven father give the Holy Spirit to them that ask him" Luke 11:13.
6. Jesus says "Ask and ye shall receive" John 16:24.
7. Jesus says "if ye shall ask anything in my name, I will do it' John 14:14.
8. Jesus says "ye have not, because ye ask not" James 4:2.

If we can understand what prayer is- prayer is asking something definite from God. The Bible says, Prayer is, asking, seeking, knocking, that is asking for something. And it shall be given to you, seek ye shall find, knock and it shall be opened unto you, for every one that asketh receiveth and he that seeketh findeth and to him that knocketh, it shall be opened" (Matt. 7:7-8). The bible says that it is not by fighting or warring or desiring or worrying but it is asking that gets things from God.

PRAISE IS BLESSED

Prayer is not praise, though praise is blessed. "Whose offered praise glorified me" (Psalm 50:23). "Let everything that hath breathe praise the Lord "(Psalm 150:6). David says "Bless the Lord, my soul and all that is within me, bless his Holy name" (Psalm 103:1). It is the duty of every grateful heart to praise the Lord. But we should remember that praise is not prayer.

ADORATION IS GOOD

Prayer is not adoration. Adoration is good. We ought to adore God whom the angels adore. But adoration is not prayer, prayer is asking.

MEDITATION IS NOT PRAYER

It is proper to meditate day and night. In the word of God (Psalm1:2). Quite devotional and mediating upon the word of God and upon the Lord's blessing are fine.

Every Christians ought to take such times for meditation but that is not prayer. It is sin when we misuse the scriptures and pervert the truth when we call such things prayer.

HUMILIATION IS PREPARATION

It is certainly proper for Christians to humble themselves before the God. "Humble yourselves in the sight of the Lord and he shall lift you up" (James 4:10). In second Chronicle 7:14 says "if my people, which are called by name, shall humble themselves and pray" so humiliation is one thing, prayer is another thing. Humiliation is preparation for prayer. And humiliation is always proper for a Christian.

CONFESSION IS NOT PRAYER

Confession is not strictly prayer but it is good for every Christians to confess their sins. Daniel 9:4. Says "And I prayed unto the Lord my God and made my confession" and said – "Daniel prayed and made confession". Read the text which tells us of Daniels Prayer and confession all together. After confession come the brokenhearted requests of Daniel. (Daniel 9:16-19). Confession is proper but it is not prayer, prayer is asking. Going through the scripture and you will find that the scripture speaks of prayer and supplication, prayer and confession, prayer and thanksgiving.

Do you really ask God for some-things when you pray? Too many people pretend to have asked when they pray. Prayer is not a love or Solemn for a sight-seeing trip around the city. Rather prayer is an empty trailer that goes straight into the warehouse back-open, loads and comes back home with goods, many people rather, they do not ask, therefore they do not receive.

Most of our so-called prayer, is not asking. When we do not ask anything and we do not get anything, this has encouraged unbelief, has cast doubt upon God and the Bible.

Millions do not know that there is a God who is ready and willing to answer prayer. And others do not believe that prayer changes things. Heart's desire is base on honest prayer. It is proper to pray aloud. It is all right to pray in a whisper. Since prayer really comes from the desire of the heart, it may over leap the incidental matters of words and sentences.

The modern tendency to have organ music during prayer is because we are not really praying. If we say, we are seeking reverence; actually we are seeking something from God, not some appealing to the senses that will help us.

Brethren, come to God asking for what you want and go home with it. Let us really learn to pray by asking things from God.

LET CONSIDER BIBLE PRAYER

Our Lord's Prayer which is the model prayer Jesus gave his disciples in (Matthew 6:9-13). He commanded us to pray thus: Our father which art in heaven ...."

First "Hallowed be thy name" – This means I speak reverently of thee and not take thy name in vain. That is making request. Secondly "Thy Kingdom comes. Thy will be done in earth, as it is in heaven". The second coming of our Lord Christ is being revealed here. It is the prayer that John the beloved prayed by divine inspiration in Revelation 22:20.

Thirdly "Give us this day our daily bread".

Fourthly "and forgive us our debts, as we forgive our debtors"

Fifthly "And lead us not into temptation.

Sixty "But deliver us from evil" and finally "for thine is the Kingdom. And the power and the glory forever". Amen.

The Lord's Prayer is a petition all the way. We are plainly commanded to pray like daily. When the scripture talks of prayer, it always means asking. Jesus gave example of prayer as one who is knocking at a door and saying "friend, lend me loaves of bread or a child asking the father fish or money. According to savior prayer is a very simple business and anybody who can ask for things can pray. People really asked for what they wanted, people who prayed in the New Testament and them revival things. Examples are:

1. Peter when he was about to sink in the waters of Galilee, Cried out "Lord, save me" (Matt. 14:30).
2. Bartimaus the blind by the roadside cried out 'Jesus, thou son of David, have mercy on me" (mark 10:47) He demanded a definite answer to his prayer by saying "Lord, that I might receive my sight (Mark 10:51). And he immediately receives his sight.

In New Testament, the only prayer that was recorded that is held up to storm is the prayer of the Pharisee in Luke chapter 18. The Pharisee

Prayed in public long and loud bit he did not ask for anything and nothing was provided for him. These are the kind of a prayer God hates.

We are so weak and sinful and God is so strong and mighty and gracious, that the only possible relationship that would be righteous and proper between us and God is that we should be asking and should be giving. When man becomes occupied with how much he can do for God, it is blasphemy and unbelief. But when poor, self confessed sinners begin to call on God for what he so graciously and lovingly offers, then, that is prayer and legitimate prayer.

Dear Pastor, test your public prayer by this measurement: was your prayer answered? God expect an answer or require one? Because pastors are accustomed with prayers of going through well-planned, pious speech which includes praises adoration, thanksgiving and even theology. It is in most cases addressed more to the people than to God. Its aim is to create a relevant atmosphere, to comfort the people and edify them. And these aren't really to get things from God. Most preachers believe that God answers prayer.

However, how sad God must be over our perversion of the doctrine of prayer and ever our failure to ask anything from God. Our prayer sometimes do very little praying, sometimes praise God, sometimes exhort the people, sometimes simply go through a form of beautiful and eloquent word, without any special heart feeling or crying out to God for anything definite.

Beloved brethren, I besiege you in the name of Jesus Christ, when you come to pray, ask things of God. Bring your wants, wishes and desires before God. Make definite requests and expect definite answer of blessings. God is rich with blessings that he longs to give and he but wait for us to ask that he give.

DON'T BE AFRAID TO ASK: GOD IS GIVER OF GOOD THINGS

Some people have so grievously doubted in regard of the power of the Holy Spirit, that many Christians fear to ask for his presence and power.

Many preachers and teachers fear to speak upon certain passages of scripture, lest they be misunderstood and accused of teaching fanaticism. But Christ knew the doubts that would arise in people's hearts when he gave this teaching on prayer and he answered your doubts.

Beloved, you need not fear to ask for bread for sinners. Christ will not give you an evil Spirit or a false testimony. Christ will not turn you over to folly. You may ask, unafraid, knowing that when you ask for bread you will get bread and not stone or you will get an egg and not a scorpion.

Hear these tender assurances of the Lord. "If a son shall ask bread of any of you that is a father, will you give him a stone? or if he ask a fish, will he for a fish give him a serpent? Or if he shall ask an egg, will he offer him a scorpion? or if ye then being evil, know how to give good gift unto your children, how much more shall your heavenly Father give the Holy Spirit to them that ask him. (Luke 11:11-13). You, weak and ignorant and sinful as you are, would not betray the confidence of your Child. You would not give a poisonous snake instead of fish, nor a scorpion nor stinging lizard to the little child who confidently pled for an egg.

So, Jesus reminds us. "If ye then, being evil, know how to give good gifts unto your children, how much more shall your Heavenly Father give the Holy Spirit to them that ask him".

We may feel perfectly safe to wait on God. Do not be discouraged. Do not listen to the taunts of those who say it is unnecessary, but ask and receive the power of the Holy Spirit.

How many preachers and Teachers hate the idea of praying for Holy Spirit. They are willing to pray for revivals, pray for the conviction of sinners, pray for power on their preaching, even pray for divine wisdom in their messages and yet they fear to pray for the Holy Spirit himself, who really brings revivals, converts sinners, who give wisdom, power and leadership to the man of God.

When we pray, we really need the power and wisdom of the Holy Spirit of God to come upon us and enable us to do what otherwise we could not do. We need the Holy Spirit of God to make us faithful soul winning. Jesus is not here teaching the disciples to pray for indwelling of the Holy Spirit, rather he is teaching them to pray for the soul-winning power of the Spirit.

According to DR Scofied, any informed man would say that every Christian has the soul winning power of the Spirit.

And that is what Jesus here again urges us to pray for. We are to pray with Holy Spirit begging, with urgent pleading, that the Holy Spirit of God will help us carry the bread of life to sinners and believers. The disciples of Jesus Christ were never taught to pray for the indwelling of the Holy Spirit and if they had prayed for his indwelling, their prayer would not have been answered.

Jesus plainly stated in (John 7:37-39), that the Holy Spirit would not be given in the sense of making his headquarters in the Christian's body until Christ should be glorified, that is, raised from the dead. Jesus command Christians should pray for the Holy Spirit to anoint us or fill us or empower us, to make us soul winners. That the Holy Spirit of God would enable us to carry the bread of life to sinners. And that is the only way soul winners are made. John 20:22 says, "Receive ye the Holy Spirit". Do not allowed anybody steal this precious verse away from you. God still give the Holy Spirit in soul winning power to those who ask him importunately and will not take "No" for an answer.

Beware brethren, let not anyone steal away the riches of the bible from you by having a man tell you that part of the bible is out of date and was not meant for you. God is still eager to have bread taken to sinners. Friends in their journey through life come to you and you have nothing to give them. But God has bread enough for all of us and will give it, if you knock at his door with importunity.

There is a way to power to fruit-bearing, you, too may enter into the miracle- working power of the Holy Spirit in saving sinners. It is not a light and frivolous matter, it is not gained by flippant or half-hearted praying. The power of the Holy Spirit is real and definite and we may know whether or not the breath of God is on us to win sinners.

We may know whether or not we have bread for sinners. We may have the bread, if we mean business but I want you to know there is a price to pay. You may have the bread if you are willing to knock at the door and wait before God until he gives you as many loaves as you need. And while you pray and wait God Will search out your heart, will show what displease him, will bring you to confession and forsaking of sin, will help you count the heavy cost. Whatever needs fixing, God can fix in your life and heart, as you wait and plead for bread of sinners, that is, the power of the Holy Spirit to win sinners.

CHAPTER FOUR

WHAT TO PRAY FOR

Jesus commands Christians to pray for our daily bread, not only bread but all our food and material necessities: God commanded us not to lay up for ourselves treasurers on earth. "take no thought for your life, what ye shall eat or what ye shall drink not yet for your body, what ye shall put on" (Matt. 6:25). That he remanded us that our heavenly father feeds the birds of the air and clothes the lilies of the field". No doubt that the savior intended us to pray for bread and clothes and all the materials blessings. All our physical needs are matters to be taken up with our Heavenly father in trusting to prayer.

The necessities of praying for are food drink and clothes. These are the matters to be freely taken up between a child and his father, between a Christian and his heavenly father. God is definitely interested in the comfort and welfare of his people. How many wonderful miracles God has worked, recorded throughout the bible, simply to give people necessary food. God willingness to give daily bread that he had for the children of Israel put a pot of manna in the Holy of Holies to keep through the centuries as a reminder of God's willing and loving providence (Exodus 16:32-4). God fed Elijah with raven (1 Kings 17:3-6) God miraculously multiplied handful of meal in a barren and the bit of oil in a cruse to feed his prophet and widow and her son, (1 Kings 17:9-16). In time of discipleship, he said to Simon" Lunch out into the deep and let down your nets for a draught". (Luke 5:4-8). Jesus fed five thousand and four thousand respectively with bread in different occasions.

Paul rejoiced because "my God shall supply all your needs accordingly to his riches in glory by Christ, Jesus. (Philippians 4:18, 19). Paul took this food as being sent from God and premised that these beloved saints who cared for God apostle should likewise have all their needs provided.

I have met the sin of unbelief as regards God's willingness to give physical blessings. Frequently people discussed in places that, "Earthly blessing were for the Jews but God gives to Christians heavenly blessings. "This is a wicked invention belief which is not certainly true".

God is willing to give daily bread to Christians in the new and Old Testament. His plan has never changed. In James 1:17 we are told "Every good gift and every perfect gift is from above and cometh down from the father of lights, with whom is no variableness, neither shadow of turning". On the matter of supplying Christian's needs, God never varies, that is never a shadow of turning away from his goodness in providential case for his own. I know that God gives great spiritual blessings in answer to prayer, but I am equally sure that he longs to give us our daily bread and raiment and to supply all our physical and material needs.

Let no one think that to pray for materials things marks one as less spiritually minded. No, the opposite is the true.

One who gets his prayers answered about daily bread will more likely pray for the salvation of sinners and will more likely get what he prays for. If God loved us enough to let Jesus die for us, he loves us enough to answer our payers and gives us all things needed even materials things.

I feel impelled to give my personal testimony and to say our God answers prayer about material things, such as food, clothes, money, jobs, cars etc. David said "This poor man cried and the Lord heard him" (Psalm 34:6). This writer says with him (David) in the agreement that "The young lions do lack and suffer hunger but they that seek the lord shall not lack any good thing" (Psalm 34:10). I think, it will glorify the

Lord and encourage the saints for me to tell briefly some of the things that God has done for me in answering prayer about material things.

When I was looking for accommodation, my wife and I call on God to remember his word in Psalm 20:1-3 which say "the lord hear thee in the day of trouble, the name of the God of Jacob defend thee, send thee help from the sanctuary and strengthen thee out of Zion and remember all thy offerings and accept thy burnt sacrifice". The Lord is a refuse, he will never allow his children suffer what is more than them. God provided the accommodation, even when our money was paid to a wrong agent, the money was retrieved which has never happened before.

Likewise, when I faced serious sickness many people have been suffering with (Diabetic) my own story was different; God make away of escape for me in answer to prayer. I remember my education, how God provided for me, I give God the glory, most of the time God made available funds for tuition and friends for logistics.

Solemnly, I tell you brethren that the definite provision of God for our needs is a regular and unfailing thing and that literally thousands of prayers, for particular definite material needs have been answered.

Oh, May God teach us to pray for our hearts, in sincere faith.

It is the will of our loving Heavenly father that we should be able to come to him day by day, ask what we want and receive it. A Christian ought to be content for the will of God to be done and to be satisfied with anything God gives. Bible promises clearly teach us to expect God to give us just what we ask for when we pray aright. A genuine answer to prayer is getting what you ask for.

THE RESULT OF DESIRED PRAYER

We are told in James 4:2 "ye have not because ye ask not". Many scripture show us that prayer in the bible sense is asking God definitely for something.

Now there is another side of that truth. If prayer is asking, then the answer to prayer must be receiving. This is the result of prayer. If we will be able to come to our heavenly father day by day, ask what we want and receive it. Jesus said "Ask and it shall be given you, seek and ye shall find, knock and it shall be opened into you, for every one that asketh receiveth and he that seeketh findeth and to him that knocketh it shall be opened. If asking is prayer, then receiving is the answer to prayer. In words of Jesus, if seeking is prayer, then finding is the answer to prayer, if knocking is prayer, and then opening door is God's answer to prayer.

Dr. Blauchard in John R. Rice (1970) says in an answer to prayer is a granting of the thing which a child asks of his Heavenly father accordingly to the directions which his father has clearly set down.

If a saint prays for healing for himself or the child or his friend and God answers his prayer, the sick person will be recovered. If a saint prays in scriptural fashion for relief from financial difficulties, he will be relived. If he prays in scriptural fashion for victory over the powers of evil, he will obtain victory. An answer to prayer is a granting of the thing desired. Saying "no" to a request is not an answer to prayer in my real, substantial meaning of the expression. When God answers prayer He says "Yes". DR Blauchard continue – Let me once more record my conviction that answered prayer is prayer which accomplishes the results desired.

If the proper answer to prayer is "Yes" answer and if a Christian who prays in a normal and scriptural manner should receive that for which he prays, then when a Christian does not get what he prays for he should begin a thorough investigation. He knows that God is not wrong. He should set out to discover by the word of God and by the leading of the Holy Spirit why his prayer has not been accepted and answered. And this makes prayer a simple and understandable business and the way to full and blessed answers to prayer will soon be open to honest, surrendered, bible-believing hearts.

CONFIDENCE IN GOD

Our relationship with God and living with him forever is more important than anything else. Christian confidence is not in themselves or what they have done or could ever do. Their confidence rests instead, totally on Jesus.

This is the confidence which we have in God, that if we ask anything according to his Will, he hears us (1John 3:14).

How do we understand Christ that give us the heartfelt security, we need in order to live in a hostile world? The only confidence is to trust our future to an unseen God. We should cherish love and gratitude, we should look unto Jesus and become transformed through our prayers. The result of this will increased our confidence, hope, patience and courage.

We can come to God with our joys, burdens and requests.

We can tell him we need money, we can tell him we have problems and need his intervention to heal us.

Have confidence that if we confess our sins and ask forgiveness, God will not put us on a waiting list, rather we can have confidence that we end our prayer forgiveness has become a reality. We do not desire to be saved isolation more ardently than Christ desires to save us.

Therefore we may be sure that if we offer any petition regarding our salvation, the savior will be more than ready to hear us or fulfill that request.

BEING PROTECTED

Nothing guarantees our protection from sickness, terrorism, war and natural disasters. We are guarantee that when we go to bed we will wake up the next day. Facing this, we do our best, trying to protect ourselves from these troubles, the best we can and yet in the end, our best efforts can guarantee us nothing.

Christians can draw near to the throne of God with confidence. You are protected because Jesus shed his blood for us on the Cross and because Jesus has ascended to heaven to serve there as High Priest on our behalf. The apostle says you may know and talks about assurance of salvation, they emphasized that our prayers are heard. We can have confident and we know is followed by the promise of divine protection.

When we pray for earthly blessings the answer to our prayer may be delayed or God may give us something other than we ask but not so when we ask for deliverance from sin. It is his Will to cleanse us from sin, to make us his children and to enable us to live a Holy life. Christ gave himself for our sins, that he might deliver us from this present evil world, according to the Will of God and our Father. (Gal 1:4).

"And this is the confidence that we have in him, that if we ask anything according to his Will, he heareth us and if we know that he hear us, whatsoever we ask, we know that we have the petitions that we desired of him. (1 John 5:14). If we confess our sins, he is faithful and just to forgive us our sins and to cleanse us from all unrighteousness (1 John 1:9).

Our petitions must not take the form of a command, but of intercession for him to do things we desire of him.

CHAPTER FIVE

PRAYING IN THE WILL
OF GOD – "YES ANSWER"

We all know that the average Christian does not usually get exactly what he asks for from God. His prayers are indefinite; they do not pointedly and plainly ask for concretes, definite answers. The ordinary "prayer" is not asking and it does not expect an answer of having. We have

1. Doubtless – This is the reason that so many Christians conditions nearly every request with "if it be thy will", that is doubt. We ask God to save sinners for whom Christ came to died and over whom he yearns with inexpressible longing. "If it be thy will", reducing our faith in God on What he can do to us through prayer.

2. Promises – we ask God for the things he has promised to give, the things which he longs to give, the things for which he has entreated us to ask, and then we ask and put a question mark by it. God forgive us, we put an "If" in our prayers about whether God is willing to save souls or keep his word. When we put "if" it is not a sign of submission to the will of God and it is a sign of unbelief. It is a sign of stumbling about in the dark in our prayers. With no assurance that God will hear us and give us the things

for which we ask. If you put "if", you are asking, whether God will keep his promises on us.

Do you think that God like doubt? No, does he like us to come with such unbelief, such stumbling, doubting uncertainty to ask for the things which he has promised and which he wants to give. God wants us to find out how to pray according to his will for things which can honor his great name and then he wants us to expect definite and exact answers to those prayers. He wants prayer to be on the basis of asking and receiving as simple as that of a child getting things from his father. And for "Yes" answer, kind of praying, there are certain important conditions that must be met.

1. There must be a total surrender to the will of God. There can be no happy, successful prayer life of a rebellious child of God. "Delight thyself also in the Lord and he shall give thee the desires of thine hearts" (Psalm 37:4). There can be no victory in prayer except as the heart humbly bows and says "my father, show me how to pray in thy will, I want to ask what will please thee. I want to have what you want me to have. God delights to answer the prayer of a surrendered heart, a heart wholly surrendered to his will. A prayer without first getting on the praying ground of a surrendered heart, are doomed to disappointment. Many Christians hinder the answers to their own prayers, that God would delights to answer, if it could be done to his glory without his encouraging sin. Oh how important it is that the heart should surrender to the Lord Jesus.

2. We must have a heart – understanding of God's word, so we may know the will of God. Jesus says "if ye abide in me and my words abide in you, ye shall ask what ye will and it shall be done unto you" (John 15:7). Asking for what we want, and getting it, is to depend upon our abiding in Christ and his word abiding in us. We cannot know the will of God without being familiar with

the word of God. The prosperity of a Christian in everything is conditioned upon his meditating day and night in the word of God and walking therein. It is not enough just to read the word of God but it should abide in us. We should love it, mediate in it, should absorbs it until it colors all lives and thoughts. Then when we came to ask something from God and can say honestly, "My dear Heavenly father, I have found in your word that you want me to have this and so and that it would honor thy name, you have said for me to ask for it, so I claim thy promise and believe thy word and take what thou hast promised me" then we can certainly expect the answer and get exactly what we prayed for. For instance, the sweet promise of God, if we confess our sins, he is faithful and just to forgive us our sin and to cleanse us from all unrighteousness" (1 John 1:9).

And prayer that is not based on the bible principles is not likely to be pleasing to God. Any Christian who put great emphasis on prayer and little emphasis on the word of God are usually fanatical, extremist, who may enjoy emotional ecstasy but do not always pray in the will of God and do not get, many times, the things for which they ask.

3. We need the leadership of Holy Spirit. Without the Holy Spirit guidance, our poor carnal minds would get only the bare letter of the bible and would not understand the will of God.

    Our prayer led and dictated by the Holy Spirit, reaches the heart of God and we get what we ask because the Holy Spirit "maketh intercession for the saints according to the will of God. Any prayer inspired and guided and aided by the Holy Spirit can be assured of an answer. According to (John R. Rice 1970) well said, that any prayer that begins in Heaven will certainly not be rejected there. (1 Cor. 6:19-20) says "what? Know you not that your body is the temple of the Holy Spirit which is in you, which ye have of God and ye are your own? For ye are bought with a price, therefore glorify God in your body and in your spirit which is God".

The blessed Holy Spirit makes known to us the will of Christ and calls to our remembrance what he has said in his word and teaches us all things to him and with fervent hearts meditate on God's word.

If we are led and helped by the Holy Spirit, those prayers will be pleasing to God. God can put in the hearts of Christians what he wants us to pray for, what will honor his name, what will prosper his cause, what will be for the happiness and good of his children. When we pray thus according to the will of God, we can get exactly what we pray for. Every prayer that is presented in Jesus name will be answered. "And whatsoever ye shall ask in my name, that will I do, that the father may be glorified in the son, if ye shall ask "ANYTHING" in my name, I will do it" (John 14:13-14). That is anything under heaven, ask in Jesus name, will be given. Do we always asking in Jesus name?

Do we really mean "Father, in thy word I have found that you have promised and the Holy Spirit has made clear his petition is exactly what Jesus wants. Here he puts his endorsement on the prayer and I know you will give it because Jesus wants it". I believe it is not the use of "in Jesus name" many such prayers do not get the answer they seek, which proves they are not really given in Jesus name.

With the above things in mind, there are clearly elements in getting ready to pray

1. We should surrender our own will and decide to have Gods own will whatever it is, whenever it leads and whatever it costs.
2. We should eagerly seek to find in the bible, what is the will of God, and then pray according to the expressed will of God written down on his word.
3. We strongly earnestly submit ourselves to the Holy Spirit for guidance and seek to have clear leading from hearts to what we should pray for and how.

CHAPTER SIX

HOW TO GET POWER FROM GOD

When Jesus Christ was alone praying, the disciples were with him. While his disciples were quietly waited, Jesus poured out his heart in prayer "And it came to pass, as he was praying in a certain place, when he ceased, one of his disciples said unto him --- teach us to pray, as John also taught his disciples". (Luke 11:1).

Brethren, we should teach people how to pray. Christians do not automatically become great men and women of prayer just as soon as they are born again. Prayer is an art that requires teaching. Every Pastor and teacher should set himself to training people in Christ like prayer. Let us study these verses in Luke 11:2-13, carefully and let us learn to pray as John taught his disciples and as Jesus taught his disciples to pray. And also we should learn to pray in the spirit they prayed.

The first thing is to come with the same hungry heart the disciples had and pray the same prayer. If you can, then pour your heart before God and earnestly, sincerely, pray this prayer, "Lord, teach me how to prayer". Prayer is a mighty weapon against temptation and enemy. Daily, let us call on God for bread, forgiveness, for guidance, for protection from sin, and the temptation.

Every Christian should learn to pray in the spirit of our Lords model prayer. And the entire petition included in the Lord's Prayer are personal and for oneself. Every Christian is invited to ask for bread for himself, forgiveness for himself, guidance for himself and deliverance for him, God has greater teaching on prayer that he wants to give us. This lesson is advance praying, intercessory praying, unselfish praying, Jesus means to teach us that importantly prayer is the way to power. God does not give the power of the Holy Spirit, simply because we are friends of God, because we wait before him, until we are fitted to receive his blessing. How do we expect marvelous power of the Holy Spirit of God to be given to us freely, without any confession of sin, without any weighing of motives, without any pealing with tears and without any transformation of life as we wait before God?

POWER FOR HEALING

In James 5:13-16 says "Is any among you afflicted? Let him pray. Is any trouble, let him sing Psalms. Is any sick among you, let him call for the elders of the church and let them pray over him, anointing him with oil in the name of the Lord. And the prayer of faith shall save the sick and the Lord shall raise him up and if he has committed sin, they shall forgive him. Confess your faith to one another and pray to one another; that ye may be healed. The effectual fervent prayer of a righteous man is—much".

When Jesus came down from the mount of transfiguration, there came a certain man kneeling down to him and saying "Lord have mercy on my son, for he is Lunatic and sore vexed (Matt. 17:5-16). A woman of disease with an issue of blood twelve years came behind Jesus touched the hem of his garment and yet there was a prayer in her timid heart. (Matt. 9:20).

All these and many other cases recorded in the Gospels were prayers for healing and Jesus answered these, everyone. On a number of occasions, multitudes brought their sick people to Jesus for him to heal. If the personal ministry of Jesus shows anything about his tender heart then he loves to heal the sick, he is glad to hear prayers for healing.

Certainly, sickness should be an occasion for prayer. We are commended to pray when we suffer ourselves and the elders of the church are to be called officially, too, to pray for the sick. If there were no particular and specific command, like this, to pray for healing of the sick, yet many other passages of the scripture authorize us to pray for any things, we want or need. In Mark 11:24 Jesus said "what things so ever ye desire, when ye pray, believe that ye receive them and ye shall have them". "If ye shall ask any thing in my name, I will do it" (John 14:14). That word anything certainly would cover healing of the body. If there were not a simple specific promise in the bible which mentioned healing of the sick in answer to prayer, yet any believing Christian would have a right to call on his Heavenly father for healing in the light of these generate promises clearly meant to cover every need of a Christian.

No instructed Christian can help acknowledging the power of the Lord to heal the body as well as to save the soul. He who credits the miracles to the bible, as every sincere Christian must, necessarily recognizes the healing power of God. God can heal. God has healed. God does heal. He heals in answer to prayer. He heals where there is no prayer at all by the recuperative power of nature. He has healed in answer to the prayer of the individual who was sick or of others who prayed for him. There are too many reputable testimonies at the present time to such healings to question them for a moment.

Brethren, let us make sure that we understand God's condition of healing. "The prayer of faith shall save the sick". Talk of oil, oil does not heal. The oil mentioned here is the symbol of the Holy Spirit, and is applied as such. It is hardly medicinal for, if God is sort of a physician, rather a quack will prescribe oil for all diseases.

Any man who is to serve God acceptably must serve in the power and anointing of the Holy Spirit and the oil is a symbol of the Holy Spirit. And every saved person has the Holy Spirit abiding in his body. And every Christian, if he wants healing should recognize that the Holy Spirit has a right to take charge and use this body as one dedicated wholly to God. To anoint, one with oil for healing would simply mean that the one anointed is dedicated to God and that we trust the Holy Spirit of God to heal the body. There is mutual prayer of Christians for one another without anointing of oil, yet it s prayer for healing. The anointing with oil is proper, under some circumstances but it is not the oil that heals. Neither is the oil essential. It is the prayer of faith that saves the sick. Faith is not an emotion but resting upon the revealed will of God, whether that will of God is revealed in his word or revolution of the spirit. If it is not God's will to heal, and if God's Holy Spirit does not give us any assurance that it is the will of God, then all of our will power will not create faith.

Where God gives the faith, God does the healing. The Holy Spirit come into regenerate and makes him a child of God and the same Holy Spirit abides in his body as the first fruits of salvation. The completion of his salvation will come when Jesus comes and when the resurrection of the Christian dead takes place and the bodies of living saints are changed in a moment, in the twinkling of an eye. Then it is true that bodily healing is in the atonement in the same sense that our resurrected bodies are provided for in the atonement. And then we will be done with all sin and will be perfect like Christ.

When there was no sin, there was not sickness. All disease and suffering came to mankind as result of fruit of sin. People suffer, sometimes when it is not their sin that causes the suffering. A classical example is Job. Sometimes people suffer for Christ's sake. If there had been no sin, there had been no suffering and often at least, suffering can be traced directly to the sins of the one who suffers it. So, one who asks God for healing should carefully consider whether there are sins between him and God.

Not all professed healings really happened. The facts remains that greatly exaggerated about many cases and there have been many hurtful things about the modern movements which has big public healing services. Often times, it has seemed a rocket to make money and exalt man life and has many Christians in despair since they have been taught that it is their own fault, they are not healed. Yet despite the failure of men, both in doctrine and life, there are many well thrown and blessed cases of healings, even miraculous healings, in answer to prayer and in them, every child of God can rejoice and can take refuse and courage. The evidence is overwhelming that many have been miraculously healed.

God is the same; the testimony of millions is that God has, in loving compassion answered their prayers for the healing of the sick. I too have seen the true answer to prayers for the healing of the sick. It is both adult and a joy to tell it to others.

CHAPTER SEVEN

PRAY FOR EVERY NEED

The book of Mark 11:24 says "what things so ever ye desire, when you pray". In Philippians 4:6 says. "In every-thing by prayer, let your requests be made known unto God".

Remember, brethren that we said earlier in the book that prayer is asking. In the book of Matt 7:7;8, says "Ask and it shall be given you, seek and ye shall find, knock and it shall be opened unto you, for every one that asketh, receiveth and he that seeketh findeth and to him that knocketh, it shall be opened. Anything that you have a right to want, you have right to ask for. Every Christian should take every desire to God in prayer. It is a sin to want anything that you cannot honestly pray for and you should ask God to remove the desire, if it is wrong. These are the conditions to be met when we pray.

"WHAT SHALL I ASK FOR WHEN I PRAY"?

1. The Lord said we are to ask for whatsoever we desire. We are to let our request in everything be made know, to God, by carrying everything to God in prayer. And as people have set and limited opinions about the proper manner of prayer, so they have most limited views of proper subjects for prayer. Some think it is wrong

to ask for rain, for jobs, for money or particular definite daily bread despite the savior's model of prayer. Christian has right to pray about anything and everything. "For verily I say unto you, that whosoever shall say unto this mountain, be thou removed and be thou cast into the sea and shall not doubt in his heart, but shall believe that those things which he saith shall come to pass, he shall have whatsoever he saith, therefore I say unto you what things so ever ye desire, when ye pray, believe that ye receive them and ye shall have them".

Anything in this world you want, even to the casting of a mountain into the sea, is included in the boundaries of legitimate normal prayer for a Christian.

2. Any thing you have a right to, whatever you have a right to, pray for it. If you do not have a right to pray for it, then it is wrong to want it. It is shameful and wicked to set our hearts on anything that we cannot honestly talk to God about.

3. Our heavenly father – wants to be taken into all the secrets and longings and desires of your heart. He wants no desire hidden from him but every desire turned into a prayer. "Be careful for nothing but in everything by prayer and supplication with thanksgiving, let your requests be made known unto God. And the peace of God which passeth all understanding shall keep your hearts and minds together through Christ Jesus.

Prayer is the cure for worry. Anxious care, fretting, the lined, harassed faces and the troubled hearts that come from frustrated desires and trouble uncertainty about the future, and all be done away with if you will come to God and ask him, frankly and boldly for everything you want and stay there until he answers.

4. Open the desire of our heart closed to God. Since I learned this blessed secret, it has done wonders for my own inner life. I have found that I ought to and that I may, freely take every desire of my heart to God. He wants me to pray about literally everything.

That is, I open every closed door. I have resolved before God that I will never want things that I cannot talk to God about. When I take the things to him, he curs the desires that are evil by helping me to confess them and he also gives me a blessed confidence that I have a right to ask of my heavenly father for anything in the world that I want.

Even a desire that is not according to his will, should I not tell him about it? Should I not ask him to reconcile my desires with his will? And if you take a matter to God and he shows you he does not want to give it to you, and then ask him to take that hurtful desire of which he does not approve out of your heart. If you want your prayers answered, seek to pray in the will of God, not contrary to his will. Seek to pray for thing that can please him, honor him, not for the things that grieve him or hinder his blessed business or encourage sin. To pray in the will of God does not mean asking less but more. And praying for just what God wants you to have will result in far more happiness than, if you could have everything you wished with some of it outside the will of God.

HOW DO WE HAVE CONFIDENT IN GETTING OUR PRAYERS ANSWERED?

And this is the confidence that we have in him that, if we ask any thing according to his will his hear us. And if we know that he hear us, whatsoever we ask we know that we have the petitions that we desired of him" (1 John 5:14,15). That is one reason for taking delight in the Lord in his work, his word, his will, his sweet presence through the Holy Spirits conscious communion. Another reason to your prayers answered is to delight in the God's will and be so surrendered to his loving plan that you and the Lord will see eye to eye and he can afford to risk you with anything you heart desires. That is praying in the will of God. We know the will of God largely through reading our bible. To pray in Jesus name simply means to pray in the will of God.

FAITH IN GOD

Faith is a gift of God (1 Corith 12:9). We shall try to show how to have faith in God and how to grow stronger in faith. No one can have faith in God for things not in God's will. Faith, really is a divinely given confidence that the thing asked is pleasing to God and that he will therefore give it. When we pray in the will of God, with a heart fully surrendered to his way, eager to do and have done his will and when we know by the sweet leading of the Holy Spirit and by the word of God, what is his will in the Matter of the prayer, the faith grows in the heart and confidently claims the blessing; which it knows it will please God to grant.

We, Christians, submit your will to God's will. Turn away from any rebellion, any willful wanting of your own way that displeases God. God wants you to have your heart's desires, wants you to be happy, prosperous and successful. He wants you to be filled with the Holy Spirit, to have soul-winning power and all the blessings that are bought for the Christian. The truth is that any Christian has a much right to pray as any other Christian. A situation where Christian depends on people, prophets and Pastors to pray for their burdens, thinking that prophets and pastors can get answer for them, when they cannot get an answer for themselves, as if God were more willing to hear pastors than to hear them.

What can make your prayer not answered can be the same reason for someone else, could not get a prayer answered for the same thing. If there is a hindrance in your life, then that hindrance would still block the answer to your prayers, doubtless, even if many others devout Christians should join in prayer for the thing you wanted for yourself.

SPECIFIC PRAYER

In any matter of daily living, we make our requests definite. We never go into a restaurant and say "Bring me some food", or no woman ever goes into a store and says, "Please give me a basket of groceries", rather she selects a certain brands. We are very definite in making our requests known about other matters.

The modern idea and modern practice about prayer is to be definite. Indefinite prayer is sally and wicked. Prayer is very definitely asking God for something. It ought to be as specific as sick man's calling a doctor, as a housewife's giving an order to the grocaryman, as an unemployed man's asking for a job etc. God wants the Christian to ask for exactly what he wants that day. This means that the Christians who are in the will of God should be expected often to have these prayers answered the same day he prays. There are many marvelous truths in this promise, but note Jesus certainly meant that a Christian have certain definite desires in his mind when he prays and then ought to be able to trust in God and get exactly those things from God which he requests. Genesis 24:12-14 says "And he said O Lord God of my master Abraham, I pray thee, send me good spend this day and shew kindness unto my master Abraham. Behold I stand here by the well of water and the daughters of the men of the city come out to draw water and let it come to pass, that the damsel to whom I shall say, let down they pitcher, I pray thee, that I may drink and she shall drink and I will give thy carnels drink also, let the same be she that hast appointed for thy servant Isaac and thereby shall I know that thou hast showed kindness unto my master". We are told Rebecca came out and offered the water and succeeding events proved she was God's answer to his and Abraham's prayer. If men and women should pray as definite about mates today, in the same spirit, no doubt God would guide them, just as clearly too happy marriage under his clear guiding.

This knowing exactly what you want and asking it, demanding it, expecting it, and knowing that it is the perfect will of God to give, it seems to be God's will for Christians. Thus said the Lord, the Holy one of Israel and his maker, ask me of things to come concerning my sons and concerning the work of my hands command ye me" Isaiah 45:11).

Blessed is to Christian who is so in the will of God, who so knows the mind of God, who has such definite desires that concerning the word of God, he can commend God and have exactly what he asks.

UNSPECIFIC PRAYER

A little consideration will be show that unspecific prayer not only fails to get things from God but shows a sinful state of heart that must greatly grieve God. Indefinite prayer is often a mere formality and is in – sincere. Many people pray day after day for things that they do not desire. Some people pray to be heard of men, not asking anything of God and not getting anything. Definite prayer is prayer that comes out of the depths of my heart not because I invented it, but because God the Holy spirit put in there and gave it such a living force that I could not help letting it out. Though such words are broken and your sentences disconnected, if your desires are earnest, if they are like coals of juniper burning with a vehement flame, God will not mind how they find expression. If you have not words, perhaps you will pray better without them, than with them, there are prayers that break the backs of words. They are too heavy for any human language to carry. Indefinite prayer usually reveals that there is no burden, no urgency in the heart. A situation where there is no definiteness in prayer. It is because there is no urgency, no real burden, and no heart desire. When we pray God want our fallow ground broken up. Indefinite prayer is prayer with no burden. One of the worst things wrong with indefinite praying is that it proves, we have not found the will of God so we do not know exactly what we should pray for. "The spirit also helpeth our infirmities, for we know not what we should pray for as we ought, but the Spirit itself maketh intercession for us with growing which cannot be uttered. And he that searcheth the hearts knoweth what is in the mind of the spirit, because he maketh intercession that suits according to the will of God. (Rom. 8: 26, 27). Nothing is dearer in the bible than those men of God who get wonderful answer to prayer which were led by the spirit of God.

They were definite in their praying because they knew what to pay for. They know what they wanted and they knew that God was willing to give these definite things. Indefinite prayer proves insincerity, our formality, proves no burden, no real heart desire in our prayers and it also proves that we have not found the will of God, have not made ourselves familiar with his plans by the word of God and by the "Holy Spirit's leading.

CHAPTER EIGHT

CONDITIONS FOR PRAYER AND IMPORTANT OF FAITH

Let me emphasis here, to you the importance of faith. You will see that faith is the very first requirement for coming to God and no one can please God without it, we are commanded to have faith in God, what unbelief is there as a wicked Sin, rebuked by the savior, which all should confess and forsake penitent hearts that everything God has promised is in answer to the prayer of faith.

In Hebrews 11:6 says "But without faith it is impossible to please him, for he that cometh to God must believe that he is and that he is a rewarder of them that diligently seek him.

Brethren, unless you believe that there is a God and also unless you believe he really hears prayers. Faith is the first requirement for everyone who would do anything, pleasing to God.

CONDITIONS OF FAITH

There is no way, you can please God without having the following attach to your faith.

1. Without faith you cannot be saved
2. Without faith you cannot pray acceptably

3. Without faith you cannot live victoriously
4. Without faith you cannot be pleasing to God in anywise.

FAITH IS COMMANDED AS A DUTY TO MAN

Jesus told his disciples to have faith, even mountains could be removed and cast into the sea by faith, thou could has whatsoever things they desired of their believe. Jesus said to Thomas "Reach hither thy finger and behold my hands, thrust it into God side and be not faithless but believing" (John 20:27).

ENLARGMENT OF PRAYER

Do you want something from God? Prayer gets things from God and the one great condition of getting things is asking for them. Bibles give special promises for those who ask in faith while others mention that we can get things we want, if we ask according to the will of God. Also we are told that whatsoever we shall ask in Christ's name, we shall have it. Scripture says unless, if two are agreed, they can have what they ask. Persistence in prayer is encouraged to and these who cry day and night to God will be heard speedily. All these are enlargements of promise not limitations. These are to make prayer easier not harder.

Ask in faith- "According to you faith so be it unto you (Matt. 9:29). "very I say unto you, if ye have faith as a grain of mustard seed ye shall say unto this mountain remove hence to yonder place and it shall remove and nothing shall be impossible unto you (Matt. 17:20). And also Matthew 21:22 says "And all things, whatsoever ye shall ask in prayer, believing, ye shall receive". "If thou canst believe, all things are possible to him that believeth" (Matt 9:23). So every Christian should dwell on this promise and as far as he is able claim them. Nothing can be clearer than that faith can get all that God has to give. Faith can get anything that God has. The most comforting example in the bible is the acts of apostle chapter 12. There you see group of some Christians spending the night in prayer at the home of Marry, the Mother of Mark. Peter, the Apostle is in prison and is to be slain tomorrow. The wicked Herod has already killed James the brother of John, to please the wicked Jews; he is willing to kill Peter too.

You can imagine their hearts were very heavy in the midst of their prayers for it seemed impossible for Peter to get out of jail. That is sixteen soldiers were on constant guard over this one man in the locked jail. Peter was even sleeping between two soldiers and was bound wick two chains. But God heard their prayers. He sent his angel who woke up Peter, broke off the chains, opened the doors and brought Peter out into the city. The truth is that asking fulfils the requirement of faith. "For whosoever shall call upon the name of the Lord shall be save".

How then shall they be save, on him in whom they have not believed? And how shall they believe in him of whom they have not heard? And how shall they hear without a preacher". (Rom. 10:13).

No one calls on God unless he believes there is a God who answers prayer. No one ask anything of this God who answers prayer unless he has some reasons to hope that even his own prayer will be answered. A Christian's faith is weak, where he can only grow is on his knees and waits before God. The place to grow faith is the place of prayer. God children go more by their wants and seeming needs than by a perfect understanding of the resources and plans of their parents. And so we frail children of God have right to come in our ignorance, in our poverty, in our littleness and unworthiness to ask God all we want and all we need. We have been taken into God's own family. We are the dear children of his heart. God's has bought us to himself at such infinite price in the death of his son that it is shameful and worked to think he would be reluctant in his giving or unwilling to answer prayers.

WHAT HINDRANCES OUR PRAYERS?

Can prayer get hindrances out of way of child of God? And so, God will hear our prayers? Yes, undoubtedly, honest, earnest asking will leads to the cure of everything that is wrong with our prayers. For example we are told wrong relationship between wife and husband hinders prayer. Being unreconciled, unforgiveness to our brothers they sin, unrepented, unlamented, unforeseen, turns away God's face and hinders our prayers? Where will God remind you of the hindrances to your prayer? It is the place of prayer. If you want God to show you what is wrong then try to pray.

Nowhere in the world is the conscience, as alive as in the place of prayer? How many times I have found that I did not know anything was wrong between me and my God, until I began to pray. There the blessed spirit of God starts to point out the things that were wrong. If you really want to know what is wrong between you and God, draw near to God and begin to pour out your heart. Be honest with God and he will be honest with you, if there are things grieving his spirit, if there are things that block his blessed he will tell you or reveal what it is. Where else would be the better place to have things made right than in the secret closeth of prayer?

Brother, sister, opens your heart honesty to the searchlight of the Holy Spirit. God's finger will surely press upon the sore spot, if you are really trying to find his will and get his blessing.

It is wonderful how prayer, the honest, earnest, surrendered, loving, persistent prayer, can remove every hindrance between man and God and cure all the ills of our poor fail Christian lives.

Brethren, I would not wait until I got everything fixed. I would not wait until I grew in faith. I would not wait until I had the victory. Come and pray, as you are keeping on praying and waiting on God, not until God gives you the faith you need, not until God modifies your prayer, God will increase your faith to fit his plan.

CHAPTER NINE

GOD HEALS SICK IN ANSWER TO PRAYER.

As we are earlier discussed about healing as it relate to our faith and how willingly the savior answered our prayers and healed the sick.

This chapter dwell exclusively how faith can heal the sick and some of bible examples to strengthen your faith.

HOW MANY TIMES OUR SAVIOUR HEALED THE SICK?

Jesus Christ in his earthly ministry had healed many people and heard the cry of the sick. The bible say in James 5:13-16, "Is any among you afflicted? Let him pray. Is any merry, let him sing psalms. Is any sick among you? Let him call for the elders of the church and let them pray over him, anointing him with oil in the name of the Lord. And the prayer of faith shall save the sick and the Lord shall raise him up and if he had committed sins, they shall forgive him. Confess your faults one to another and pray one for another, that ye may be healed. The effectual fervent prayer of a righteous man availed much".

Brothers and Sisters, this is where our faith lies. If there were not a line in the bible upon which to base our hope except this –is sufficient to raise our faith on God concerning the answer to prayers. He made it known repeatedly that without faith it is impossible to please God and faith worked to those who believe in him, that is, where healing takes place.

God is our heavenly Father and we are his dear children, redeemed at infinite cost, then surely that alone would give us a right to look up in his face and tell him of our woes and ask him for help in our sufferings and sickness.

As Jesus himself went about doing well and was moved with compassion by the sickness and the sorrows of the people, so he has compassion upon us now and our dear heavenly Father has loving compassion upon his children. "Like a Father pitied his children, so the Lord pitied them that fear him (Ps 103:13).

Jesus was willing to answer the prayer of the sick such as a Leper said to Jesus, "Lord, if thou welt, thou canst make me clean". (Matt 8:2), a Capernaum said, "Lord, my servant lied at home sick of the palsy, grievously tormented. (Matt 8: 6). And a certain ruler worshiped Jesus saying, "My daughter is even now dead, but come and lays thy hand upon her and she shall live". (Matt 9:27)

There come also a woman of Canaan, cried to Jesus saying "Have mercy on me, O Lord, thou son of David, my daughter is grievously vexed with a devil (Matt 15:22). A woman diseased with an issue of blood twelve years came behind Jesus touched the hem of his garment, and yet there was a prayer in her timid heart. (Matt 9:20).

Finally, when Jesus came down from the mount of transfiguration, there came a certain man kneeling down to him and saying, "Lord, have mercy on my son for he is Lunatic and sore vexed, for often times he falleth into the fire and often into water.

All these and many other cases were recorded in the bible, as were prayers for healing and Jesus answered these, everyone. On a number of occasions, multitudes brought their sick people to Jesus for him to heal. Jesus shows everything about his tender heart, then, he loves to heal the sick, he is glad to hear prayers of healing.

SICKNESS IS AN OCCUSSION FOR PRAYER

"Is any sick among you, let him call for the elders of the church and let them pray over him. And the prayer of faith shall save the sick and the Lord shall raise him up". Invariably sickness should be occasion for prayer. We are commanded to pray when we suffer ourselves and the elders of the church are to be called officially too, to pray for the sick. In James 5:16, we are told "Confess your faults one to another, and pray one for another, that ye may be healed.

Though the sick may pray for themselves, it is proper for the elders of the church to pray also and individual, Christians are to confess their sins one to the other and to pray one for the other, in order that they may be healed.

If there were no particular and specific command, like this, to pray for healing of the sick, yet many other passages of scripture authorize us to pray for anything we want or need. For instance, the book of Mark 11: 24, Jesus said, "what things so-ever ye desire, when ye pray, believe that ye receive them and ye shall have them". That is what things so ever would certainly include the healing of our sick bodies. And in John 14:14, Jesus promised, "If ye shall ask any thing in my name, I will do it," That word anything certainly would cover healing of the body.

In Philippians, we are instructed to "...in everything by prayer... let your requests be made unto God". If there were not a single specific promise in the bible which mentioned healing of the sick in answer to prayer yet any believing Christian would have a right to call on his Heavenly Father for healing in the light of these general promises, clearly meant to cover every need of a Christian. Sickness and disease come from Satan. God permits them as he permits sin and permits certain results of sin. And often God overrules sickness to his own glory. Surely, the very nature of sickness means that we ought to pray about it and have a perfect right to pray about the healing of our bodies.

Christians ought to pray alone when they are sick. Christians should call their pastors or church officials to pray. It is perfectly legitimate to have prayer in public services, just so if it is sincere prayer God-honoring the prayer and not one connected with false doctrine. Christians should pray privately for one another, confessing their faults one to another. Sickness is a proper subject for prayer.

Brethren, we sinned in not looking first to the Lord, when we sick instead we trusted men. The bible never indicates that it is wrong under certain circumstances to use doctors and medicine. But we may be sure; it grieves God when his children think first about human help and human remedies. The very first thing anybody should do about sickness is to pray.

DO YOU SHARE TESTIMONIES?

Dear friend, when last do you give or share testimony with your beloved fellow Christians? Do you know that given testimony grieve Satan? Testimony sharing restore you back to God, glorify the name of God and give others hope and recall those who have lost and strengthen the faith of hopeless. And testimony sharing always grieves Satan to be unhappy. Do you know that Satan always trembles when he sees smallest Christian knee before God? Only, if we can call God first or invite him first when we sick or other things in our life.

A Dear Christian sister called me "Bro Ogogo, if the time ever comes when I am sick and the doctors can't help me and when medicine don't work, I am going to try and call on you and our church to pray for me". This happen to the rest of us that is, we call on God when other things have failed. How glad would it be when you call on God first? As he may directs, we can use medicine and doctors as he leads and give God the glory when he heals. He gives faith for healing without doctors and medicine; we can take the blessing he gives and thank him for it.

Christians should look first to God in every trouble and in every need. So when Christians are sick, we should pray and others should pray for us too.

No doubt there are many Christians who are sick who ought to be well and would be if they came in Jesus' name to God in prayer according to the scriptural plan. In those cases where it is not God's will to heal the sick, he will make his Will know to humble and surrendered hearts. So whenever we are sick, let us pray for the Will of God to direct.

THE PRAYER OF FAITH SHALL SAVE THE SICK

There are conditions stipulated by God to heal. He says "the prayer of faith shall save the sick". The book of Divine Healing authored by DR.R.A Torrey, call attention to the fact that it is not attending three days night vigil service but it is the prayer of faith that saves the sick. In the book of Leviticus 8:10-12, shows that alter, vessels and its base were all anointed and sanctify them. Any man who is to serve God acceptably must serve in the power and anointing of the Holy Spirit. And every saved person has Holy Spirit abiding in his body.

And every Christian, if he wants healing should recognize that the Holy Spirit has a right to take charge and use this body as one dedicated wholly to God. To anoint one with oil for healing would simply mean that the one anointed is dedicated to God and that we trust the Holy Spirit of God to heal the body, if it is God's Will.

In Romans 8:11, says "But if the Spirit of him that raised up Jesus from the dead dwell in you, he that rose up Christ from the dead shall give life also to your mortal bodies through his Spirit that dwelled in you".

There is mutual prayer of Christians for one another, without anointing of oil, yet it is prayer for healing. Anointing with oil is sometimes a help to our faith. It reminds us that the Holy Spirit of God dwells in the body of the sick Christian. Whether, we use oil or not, it is the prayer of faith that saved the sick.

In the bible there is no mention of anybody's anointed with oil except elders of the church. Christians has a right to pray for their own healing or for the healing of a friend or loved one.

Modern evangelists who have so-called "divine healing services" and say that it is always God's Will to heal, sometimes lays the blame for their failures on those who come to be healed. When the disappointed sick person is not healed, the evangelist disclaims all responsibility and says that the sick person simply did not have faith in God or that some other sin was responsible.

In 1 Corinth's 12:8, 9, says "For to one is given by the Spirit the word of wisdom, to another the word of knowledge by the same Spirit, to another faith by the same Spirit". The Holy Spirit gives faith. When God's word has a plain promise to us, it would be sin not to believe the promise and risk God. We must depend upon the Holy Spirit to show us the Will of God. If God's Holy Spirit gives us faith for healing, then our prayer for healing will be answered.

But if it is God's Will to heal and if God's Holy Spirit does not give us any assurance that, it is the Will of God, then all our will power will not create faith. Where God gives the faith, God does the healing. Where God is not pleased to heal in a particular case, he will not give faith for healing.

Faith is not an emotion but a resting upon the revealed Will of God. Whether, that Will of God is revealed in his Word or by revelation of the Spirit. Sometimes people say they have faith when they are depending upon the Word of Preacher. The Holy Spirit makes us sure that it is his Will to do the thing we ask, then, we have God given faith and we can claim the answer and expect it.

THE WILL TO HEAL IN ANSWER TO PRAYER

Before anyone can come to pray for healing, either for himself or for another must comes saying, "Nevertheless not as I will, but as thou will" (Matt26:39). Before we can depend on God or claimed healing, we must first have surrendered hearts, be ready to have sickness. We also know that percentage of sick people would get well without a physician or medicine. God put healing forces in nature and the body itself tends to combat diseases. That shows clearly that health is God's plan.

We know that God's great compassion and love toward his children is greater than that of an earthly father, he never wants us to suffer except when it is for our own good and for his own glory. "He who, spared not his own son but delivered him up for us all, how shall he not with him also freely gives us all things". (Rom 8:32). All things are truly good and for our happiness and welfare.

But in the great majority of cases, where Christians seemed honestly to forsake their sins and wait on God to find God Will about sickness, healing is the normal and to be expected thing for a Christian who is in the Will of God. A Christian should be hungry, sometimes be out in cold without a bed or be in sun or without sufficient clothes for the sake of Christ. We should be willing to suffer for him.

Paul, Peter and many others of the best Christians have suffered these things. But usually that is not God's Will. Christians should pray for and get their daily bread and sufficient clothing. So Christians should learn how to go earnestly and confidently to God in prayer every time they are sick and ask for healing. Unless God does reveal that he has other plans after we earnestly seek to know his Will and to make it ours, then we have right to wait confidently on God for healing, provided we confess and forsake our sins and seek his face with a surrendered heart.

What God wants, I am sure is for Christians to pray and follow his leading, then trust in him to lead, using human means and our best wisdom or if he so leads, trusting him to heal without Medicine and Doctors. What is important, whether with Medicine or without, it is God who does the healings? He should have all the glory; our trust should be in him all times, not in men.

CONFESSED AND FORSAKE SIN

When there was no sin, there was no sickness. All diseases and suffering came to mankind as the fruit of sin. People suffer, sometimes when it is not their own sin that causes the suffering. Job is a classic example. People suffer for Christ's sake. But if there had been no sin, there had been no suffering; at least suffering can be traced directly to the sins of the one who suffers.

So, one who asks God for healing should carefully consider whether there are sin between him and God.

MARVELLOUS ANSWERS TO PRAYER FOR HEALING SICK

Not all professed healing really happened. The facts have been greatly exaggerated about many cases and there have been many hurtful things about the modern movement which has big public healing services. Often it has seemed a racket to make money and to exalt man and has left many Christians in despair or a state of limbo, since they have been taught that it is their own fault they are not healed. Despite the failure of men, both in doctrine and life, there are many well-known and blessed cases of healings, even miraculous healings in answer to prayer and in them every child of God can rejoice and can take courage. The evidence is overwhelming that many have been miraculously healed.

God is the same, Jesus Christ is the same. The testimony of millions is that God has, in loving compassion answered their prayers for the healing of the sick.

This happened to my own daughter, when she was four years old, had a cough which clipped her throat. We carefully attended to her at home, but when after a few days her throat seemed worse and combined with fever. We took her to our family doctor for examination and her temperature and pulse, it was amazing. When we returned home and put the child on bed, I said to my wife, let us invite God into this case because I have been telling people that God answers prayer and now I am going to pray for my own. I kneel by my bed side and stay there until I have assurance from God that Nnenna will get well and that he has taken complete charge of the case. My wife too said, she would do the same.

We knelt in prayer, remembering that he who knee before the Lord will stand among men. We start reminding God of how we had given the child to him when we she was born, reminding God of his promises and telling him that if he would heal her, we would praise him and would give him the glory instead of the doctor and would earnestly try to raise the child for him. Soon I felt assured that God had heard us. My wife felt the same way. We rose from our knees after thanking God.

That afternoon the fever went down, that night or the next day the sickness has gone entirely.

God simply kept his word that "The prayer of faith shall save the sick and Lord shall raise her up.

I do not feel that there was any merit in what I did, except that it was simple obedience and I believe that thousands of others can have as remarkable answers to prayer as that, if they only obey God's simple command and pray for the sick, believing the bible and giving God a chance prove the mightier he is.

The elders of the church should be willing to anoint the sick with oil, when it is requested in the bible manner and when they can do it in the name of the Lord. It was surprising and blessed results follow God's way, many times.

It is obvious that this book has second part which deal with the fasting and prayer.

Prayer and fasting was the Master Key that Christ used to make the impossible possible and also Master key by which we too can meet the desperate situations (Needs) of humanity and make the impossible to become possible.

In the scripture, we find out men losing their place with God through failure to control temptations of the flesh and at the same time, we find others who through the discipline of fasting over-come all obstacles and got answers of prayer from God that changed the destinies of kingdoms. Eating and drinking are not wrong unless they become an end in themselves.

We shall explain briefly the different types of fasting as recorded in, from different Prophets and Pastors in the book.

There is something that has been missing, as we believe that people who using white fasting are considered to be using total fasting and while, white fasting, as Christians that have no faith or physical fortitude to undergo fasting. These people often attempt fasting but became so weak that they are unable to continue or if they do, they are unable to pray effectively and the result is that instead of a victory, they experience a defeat. Those who are able to fast totally, God blessed them and the Lord God led them and others in more such fasts. But those great number of people who want to fast and have attempted it – in some cases, many times but have be able to accomplish little.

These are some of the questions the part 2 of this book will deliberate and attempt to answer.

- WHY DO WE FAST AND PRAY?
- WHAT CAN WE GET FROM FASTING AND PRAYER?
- PRAYERS THAT DEMANDS GREAT THINGS FROM GOD
- And many more.

I know with God all things are possible to those who believe in him.

We must remember that faith is a gift of God and the Holy Spirit will not help us to have faith about wicked things out of the Will of God. The point is quite plain here that a miracle was possible in the apostles' days in answer to the prayer of faith and that anything else in the world in any day can have a miracle on exactly the same conditions when we adopts fasting and prayer.

And then, Jesus gave the general Law of Miracles in answer to prayer when he concludes in Mark 11:24. "Therefore I say unto you, what things so-ever ye desire, when ye pray, believe that ye receive them and ye shall have them". It is a blessing to remember here specifically that miracle is an object of conversation and things he has in mind when he gave this blessed promise.

Anybody who has enough faith in Christ can do his work, the same kind of work that Jesus had been doing. Certainly, then, the savior promised miracles to those who ask things purely in his name. That is, when one can ask a thing wholly in Jesus' name or with his authority and for his sake, with his approval, then one can get it even, if it be a miracle.

CHAPTER TEN

UNVEIL YOUR PONTENTIALS (IDEAS)

Anyone can shout and rejoice after the victory but it takes faith to shout before the victory.

So, an "idea" is something that exists in the mind, the product of mental activity, a thought or a mental image, the ability to see something.

Recently, I read an article which stated that average individual has over two thousand ideas in a day pass through his mind. It could be positive or negative idea depending on which side you want to apply the idea. It is your choice to extract the useful one to your life.

After reading this article, I added up the number of new ideas I had in one month. My range was from fifteen to twenty thousand strong ideas. These ideas only came when I was in a receptive and sensitive attitude.

A few years ago God showed me from Proverbs 16.3, how to inspired idea. Roll your works upon the, commit and trust them wholly to him. (He will cause your thoughts to become agreeable to His Will and so shall your plans be established and succeed).

Even though, there is a place in your life where you may has health, abundant life and financial success. There is a place where you can achieve your goals and realize your dreams. If you can trust the works of your hand and the Lord with commitments. There is a sweet place within you.

God want to release that sweetness out of you soon. But there are wells, limitations around your sweetness Jericho.

God told Joshua, he had given him the city of Jericho, not just the walls around the city. The walls surrounding Jericho limited your entrance. Are there walls today in your life keeping you from getting into your sweet smelling place? Such as:

Resentment

Wrong thinking (ideas)

Jealousy

Unforgiveness

Backbiting

Strife

Carnality.

These walls will definitely stop you from acknowledging and harvesting the good things in your life. The angels of God are appointed to guide those who honor the Lord and rescue them from danger (Psalm 34: 7 and 91:11). Only what you need to break the walls of Jericho concerning your life., is to pray to the Lord because our Lord loves prayer whether be it in the church or with your family or in your own room, for he knows that a Christian cannot grow without communicating with God in prayer.

In order to do this, what miracles do you need right now? What is your sweet place in place in life? What are your dreams? What are your goals? Do you need a happy family, total healing and health prospering, finance, transportation, a good Job, a sound mind, a nice car? Whatever you need, your heavenly Father has the answer waiting for you. The GRAT "I am" is everything you need. When Joshua and the people followed God's instructions a exactly and shouted in faith before their victory the walls that had surrounded their sweet place in life collapsed.

As the children of Israel acted upon the word of God spoken by his servant, Joshua, they received their sweet place in life. God has given me the plan and the anointing to help you achieve your maximum potential and enter into your place of God's abundance in your life. It's the same plan that God wants us to follow today for your needs.

First, sit down right now and tell me on the enclosed prayer or what you will request on telephone or what you want from God, so that we pray together. What do you believe your sweet place in life is ? May be you need an inspired idea, a new beginning, a new car, a marriage, your children's salvation or to be released from fear. Whatever it is, call me at the end of the book with numbers to make prayer requests.

Together, we're going to believe God for a supernatural miraculous energizing of your potential. Together, we are going to sound the trumpets and have the music going forward.

I believe with all my heart that as we unite together in the praise and worship of God, the powers of darkness are going to be pulled down.

From the moment we shout your victory, miracles are going to begin to happen. Your dreams are going to stir within you and bubble forth. Things that have missing in your life are going to begin to show up from that moment. There's going to be a healing that will take place in every area of your life. It is very important that you will see your spoken word in your life come through.

You will be releasing what you have in your hands to God and receiving until there is giving, what is in God's hands for you. There is no receiving until there is giving, there is no reaping until there is sowing. When you give, you are saying, "God, I believe that I receive".

You are receiving now, what you, what been believed, I am trying to get faith released, so that you can look beyond what is seen. Joshua saw the victory. I want you to see your victory too.

Be reminded, that "whoever thinks, he is standing firm had better be carefull that he does not fall"(1 Corint 10:12) and we must put on all the armor that God gives us, so that we will be able to stand up against the devil's evil tricks (Eph 6:11-18).

Bible says, God uses foolish things to confound the wise and he uses weak things to confound the mighty (1 Corint 1:27).

But all starts with faith in God, you must see him first. Look not at the things that are seen and God said he would give the things you have need of (Math 6:33).

God is about to show himself strong on your behalf. Those abilities, ideas, talents and dreams which God has placed within you are going to supernaturally energize and change your life. Your friends and neighbors will see what is happening and they will know that your God is the almighty God that answers prayer. The end of your sorrow is near because God has a sweet, fragrant place prepared for you that have never known before.

Taste and see, the sweetness of the good things he has in store for you right now (Ps 34:8)

Brethren, what are you giving to God? You may discover that people in general want to receive all the blessings from God. All the rain and all the sunshine, but they do not want to commit themselves to serving God as their Lord and savior. And, to many God is only good enough to help in times of trouble and despair. Have you committed your life to Lord God?

Have you declared openly through (Baptism) that you have given your heart to Jesus Christ by what you say and do?. Or are you ashamed to let others know? Jesus said. "If anyone declares publicly that he belongs to me. I will do the same for him before my Father in Heaven" (Math 10:32, 33)

Our Lord Jesus said, "Whoever does not take up his cross and follow my steps is not fit to be my disciples"

TEST OF SPIRIT

Jesus gives the following invitation to everyone who is thirsty concerning spiritual matters. 'Whoever is thirsty should come to me and drink (John 7: 37, 38). 'Come everyone who is thirsty, here is water, come you that have no money- buy corn and eat. Come buy spiritual wine and milk- it will cost you nothing' (Isa 55; 1). He continued, whoever drinks water that I will give him will never be thirsty again. The water that I will give him will become in him a spring which will provide him with life- giving water and give him eternal life" (John 4: 14).

Dear brothers and sisters how do you portrait yourself at public and home? How do you act in the public or other places? How should Christian live? The live of a Christian should squarely found in (Galatians 5: 22-230 " But the fruit of the spirit is love, joy, peace, long-suffering, gentleness, goodness, faith, meekness, temperance, against such there is no law.

We are going to look at what happen to those whose lives are completely surrounded with God and who allow the Holy Spirit to work in them. The spirit is what grows in us when we are born of the spirit and what happens when we are born again.

When talking of the Holy Spirit, Apostle Paul is talking not about separate traits that operate independently of one another but about a single reality that links us or guides us when we pray and direct us what to pray for. The fruit of the spirit is what the Holy Spirit creates within us, it defines the type of person we are to become in Jesus. The spirit is like a precious jewel with many facets, characterized of Jesus and represents a quality that he wants to produce in one lives. This is the heart of the matter. God's purpose is to make us like Jesus and he has sent his Holy Spirit to dwell in us in order to make that change happen.

It is not a lifestyle, though a person who is cultivating the fruit of the spirit will not live as he or she died before. The spirit is a change of human being, old things are passed away, behold all things are become new. (2 Corinth 5:17). The fruit of the spirit is the "New" in the life of a person who has passed "from death unto life in Christ" (1 John 3: 14).

How do we become more patient or more loving or more gentle or more faithful but on how will can let the Holy Spirit make us more like Jesus who is patience, love, gentleness and faithfulness personified?

There are challenges to cultivate the grace of the Holy Spirit at all times, more especially at home. Where you will see surrender, a willingness to die to self and live for God and for others as a tree is known by its own fruit.

ADVANCED PRAYER PART 2

This book is written to bridge the gap and to encourage brethren in the Lord and people who have not taken decision to receive Jesus Christ as their Lord and personal savior. That is anything we ask through his name shall been given to us, if our will allied with the will of God.

People find it extremely difficult to get things from God because we are not following the will of God. Following the will of God means that our prayers will be answered, that is doing away those things that will not please God in our life. It is common to ask, what are those things, we want to put away in our life. The bible says, in the book of. (John 8:47) "He that is of God heareth God's words, ye therefore hear them not, because ye are not of God". See, How to knowing God at last page.

1. This book is to encourage the weak Christians to develop better understanding in our Lord Jesus Christ and to have an apple opportunity to increase our faith in your prayer life because this teaches, how to get blessing from our God and also to increase your relationship with our Lord Jesus Christ.

2. To the faithful who have understood the way to reach God and benefit from the promises of our Lord Jesus Christ. On how to grow more powers, strengthen and to do the will of God always. This book, enhances how to teach others how to be richly in God and claim the promises of God and received it, as an answered to prayers.

3. To unbelievers- This book entails you what you have been missing from God all these wiles. This is an opportunity to turn back and receive Jesus Christ. God will receive you as long as you pray through the will of God, God will forgive your sins and answer your prayers and all your lost glory will be restored back, your power will be restored because without Jesus, no power, no peace, no happiness, no abundance of life. Jesus is everything and the answered prayer is power.

4. Proclaim- that you know Jesus Christ is my Lord and my personal savior and I know God will in my life. It should show clearly how meaningful knowledge of God bringing blessing to me now and eternal life in the time to come. This is the word of God. It is best to set aside time to each day to read bible, mediate on it and talk to God in prayer. You will richly be blessed as you do this.

We pray every day in our life. We confessed our sins and thanksgiving to our almighty God for his mercies and guidance in our life.

We make prayer for our daily bread as God promised that we should ask for our daily bread as he has promised in (Mathew 7: 7-8). " Ask for your daily bread and other needs which he has promised his people".

When these prayers has transient beyond the routine prayer of daily bread and needs, it has become advanced prayer. The advance prayer we mean here are fasting and praying.

Prayer has become an advanced prayer when you have fixed a day or days or week(s) to seek the face of the Lord in prayer and with fasting. That is when prayer has transient from routine prayer into advance prayer. As you know that Jesus prayed, but when he wanted to seek the face of his Father in prayer he went into mountain with fasting and praying.

This tells us that when we are in serious situation or demand or want, we should forgo bread and become serious to seek the face of the Lord in prayer. If we want our situation to improve or to change for better or our asking or prayer to be heard, should be in fasting and praying.

CHAPTER ELEVEN

EATING AND DRINKING SPIRITUAL BARENESS

As Jesus Christ's fasted forty days and forty nights in the wilderness, he ever-come the fiercest onslaughts of the enemy, made possible the restoration of man's dominion (Luke 4: 1-13). Prayer and fasting was the Master Key that Christ used to make the impossible possible and also Master Key by which too can meet the desperate situations (needs) of humanity and make the impossible to become possible.

As the appetite uncontrolled leads to spiritual bareness and even disaster, so we shall see in this book, how true fasting and denying the appetite gives men a new grip in God.

Esau was typical example in the bible who lost his been the Father of the chosen race instead to Jacob because of appetite of mere mess pottage. Fasting reverses the order. It disciplines the soul and in its abstinence from the earthly, it opens the door to the Heavenly. In the scripture, we find out losing their place with God through failure to control temptations of the flash and at the same time, we find others who through the discipline of fasting over-come all obstacles and got answers of prayer from God that changed the destinies of kingdoms. Eating and drinking are not wrong unless they become an end in themselves.

We shall explain briefly the different types of fasting as recorded in from different Prophets and Pastors.

FASTING WITH WATER.

Ordinarily, fasting includes the drinking of water, as water is not regarded as a food, as it contains no calories, no nutrition of any kind. However, since the body is eight percent water and may lose several quarts daily by evaporation by which it maintains temperature equilibrium in the body, water is very essential to life and must be constantly replenished in the human system.

TOTAL FASTING

Total fasting excludes the eating of food and water. But can be done in this form- Any food/drink you take at the night of Sunday, you will not eat/drink anything till the evening of Monday 6.00pm. That is total fasting that works, etc.

WHITE FASTING

White fasting has more powers than ordinary fasting, for example any food/drink you have taken at night on Sunday and you must not take anything till the evening of Monday by 6.00pm. When you want to break it, you should not eat or drink, any food/drink that has salt, sugar, pepper, oil butter etc. You can drink gari with coconut, eating ripe banana, plantain or eating of boiled Yam or plantain without the materials mentioned above until the following day say (Monday-Thursday).

There is something that has been missing, as we believe that people who are using white fasting are considered to be using total fasting and white fasting as for Christians that have no faith or physical fortitude to undergo fasting.

These people often attempt fasting but became so weak that they are unable to continue or if they are unable to pray effectively and the result is that instead of a victory, they experienced a defeat. Those who are able to fast totally, God blessed them and the Lord God led them, and others in more such fasts. But those great number of people who want to fast and have attempted it-in some cases many times but have been able to accomplish little.

In this regard, many people using white fasting are under obligation to continue their daily work. They realized that it would be best for them to suspend their regular duties until after the fast but modern life is so, set up that it is almost impossible for them to do this.

Have you wonder why believers have to fight an "unending battles"?. It is not that Christ is powerlrss or unable to save, the simple reason is that refusal of such believers to engage in sound and spirit, directed warfare against the enemies of their blessing, sponsoring barriers in various dimensions.

The Lord told his children go out against them (enemies) though he said the battle is his,that is why you cannot fold your arms and be looking why devil and his agents are battling your destiny. You must rise up and fight from the victory of the cross and enforce this victory against the enemies of your life. Go up to the high places and pull down the devil's kingdom built against your progress (2 Chron 20:15-17).

Finally, Jesus Christ told us in the book of (Luke 18:12-14) that " For every one that exalted himself shall be abased and he that humblest himself shall be exalted". There is a right way to pray, a right way to worship God, a right way to exercise the gift of the spirit, so there is a right way to fast. The one that give great results may be the one obtained through the fasting and prayer.

CHAPTER TWELVE

WHY DO WE FAST AND PRAY?

Why Christians leave food, sleep, nice clothes, family life or other comforts to do nothing than pray?

Saints of God got their prayers answered when they waited on God in fasting and prayer. The greatest saints of God throughout the bible often fasted. Fasting is often connected with wholehearted prayer with mourning, with repentance, with seeking deliverance from enemies or wisdom from above. Moses fasted for forty days on Mount Sinai and our savior fasted forty days in the wilderness. Joshua, David, Paul, Anna, Ezra, the apostles, Nehemiah, the disciples, John the Baptist, Barnabas and others fasted and prayed.

Since, in the bible times, the greatest men of prayer have often times fasted as well as prayed. A Christian is in a safe hand or in good company when he fasts and prays. The disciples of John the Baptist fasted, the Pharisees fasted and naturally the disciples of our savior fasted when Jesus answered. "Can ye make the children of the bride Chamber fast, while the bridegroom is with them". But the days will come when the bridegroom shall be taken away from them and then shall thy fast in those days" (Luke 5: 34-35). The disciples of Jesus fasted after he was taken away.

The restriction that our savior put upon fasting is that it must be sincere. Saints of God must be sincere when searching the face of God in payer. Men should not disfigure their faces to appear unto men to fast. A boastful, self-righteous flaunting of righteous ceremonies such as that practiced by the Pharisees, hypocrites in the days of our Lord is offensive to God to be sure. We shouldn't fast as hypocrites. We should fast as Jesus Christ fasted and Paul and Barnabas fasted and many others men of God fasted.

WHAT IS FASTING?

Fasting means putting God first. There are times when one ought to eat and praise God for the food, as David when he said "Bless the name Lord o my soul and forget not all his benefits...... who satisfied my month with good things, so that thy youth is renewed like the eagles" (Ps 103: 2, 5). There are times, when it pleases God for his child is quietly

And trustfully to lie down to sleep, lay aside all his burdens and sweetly resting in the blossom arms of God's care. There are times when men should enjoy the pleasure of family life. "Marriage is honorable in all and the bed undefiled" (Heb 13: 4). We are told that "whoso findeth a wife findeth a good thing and obtained favor of the Lord" (Prov 18: 22).

"Every good gift and every perfect gift is from above and cometh down from the Father of lights, with whom is no variable, neither shadow for -turning" (James 1: 17). It is necessary for us to enjoy the blessings of God, whether food or drink or rest or Christian fellowship or home life or service. Let us give God the glory for them all. And again but certainly there are times when we should turn our backs upon everything else in the world to seek the face of God. Such times should be times for fasting and prayer.

Fasting determine how to seek the face of God in prayer and to abstain from other things in order to give the whole heart to prayer and waiting on God. Fasting and prayer is regarded a time, when to leave the lesser blessings for the greater one, the lesser duty for the far more important duty. Times when preachers should quit preaching and all of us should leave off bible study and go out to win the souls and in order to win the soul you must pray.

Sometimes those who fasted in the bible times fasted without any kind of drink, as well as without food. The men of Nineveh did "Not food, nor drink water" (Jonah 3:7).

Even Queen Esther and her maidens and Mordecai and other Jews, before the days of Purim, when Jews were to be destroyed by the plot of wicked Haman, they did not eat food nor drink water for three days (Esther 4: 16).

When God panned to give law to Israel from Mount Sinai, he commanded the people to wash their clothes and "come not close to your wife"

And husbands and wives were commanded, " Defraud ye not one another, except it be with consent for a time, that ye may give yourselves to fasting and praying" (1 corinth 7:5)

Fasting is really putting God first when one prays, wanting God more than one wants food, more than one wants sleeps, more than one wants fellowship with others, more than one wants to attend business. How could a Christian ever know that God was first in his life, if he did not sometimes turn aside from every other duty and pleasure to give himself wholly to seeking the face of God?

In many other occasions in life when men do without food.

For instance, like a footballer, men gladly deprive themselves of sweets and certain foods likely to hinder mental alertness and physical fitness and endurance. Should we do less for Jesus Christ? One cans run a race better, if he has not eaten just before hand. Example Swimmers alike also know that it is dangerous to eat much before swimming lest they suffer from cramps, likewise public speakers and singers customarily do not eat in the evening until after the important period of concentration and perfect control necessary for their public appearance.

If I can preach better without eating, then why can't I pray without eating? If a businessman can concentrate better on his figure in some emergency without having his stomach loaded with food, then why can't

I a Christian pray better when all his energies are given to that one thing? When men are wholly absorbed in grief for a loved one, they are not hungry. Then when one is wholly absorbed in passionate and most early prayer, why should he not be glad to do without food?

FASTING IS PERSISTENCE IN PRAYER.

Really, persistence in prayer is letting other things go and giving God the right way, often involves fasting. In fact, I think there is little point to fasting or depriving ourselves of other things, simply as a matter of self-punishment, if we do not pray. If a man is to be just as absorbed in the business as even with no more thought for God, then what good would it do his spiritually to do without food or drink or sleep?. Fasting is the accomplishment of persistence, fervent prayer that will not be denied.

Fasting is the deliberate clearing of the way for prayer, laying aside weights and hindrances. "Wherefore seeing we also are compassed about with so great a cloud of witness, let us lay aside every weight and the sin which doth so easily beset us and let us run with patience the race that is set before us looking into Jesus the author and finisher of our Faith" (Heb 12:1-2).

A Christian ought to be willing as often as necessary to abstain from anything that hinders getting the answer to his prayers, to wait on God until everything that hides the face of God is answered or removed, waiting before God until really he gets the full assurance that his prayer is heard and will be answered to the glory of God. When we fast and pray, we are simply trying to lay aside sincerely anything that hinders our prayers.

Another thing fasting stand for us is that fasting pictures greater desire, greater determination and greater faith. One who fasts thereby signifies his sincerity and his confidence that God can be reached and that God will answer and bless his sincerity and definiteness and willingness to know and do the will of God. Prayer is too often a shadow thing a light and insincere thing. That is surely one reason why so many prayers are never answered. Fasting then should be simply an evidence of our earnestness, our farvor, our faith with the Lord.

However, it is only when men have reached a place of deep humanity that they are in a position to accomplish a great work of God.

WHAT CAN WE GET FROM FASTING AND PRAYER?

Good things never come to a child of God by easy. "But by fasting and prayer". If prayer is good, then more prayer is better. If earnest prayer pleases God, then he is pleased when the prayer is so earnest that we do not want food or drink or sleep or other pleasures.

1. In times of trouble, God says "Call upon me in the day of trouble. I will deliver thee and that shall glories me" (Ps 50:15). In time of trouble is a good times to pray. If it is a good time to pray and if the trouble is sincere, then it is a good time to fast too. Joshua and the elders of Israel remained prostrate before the Ark of God from morning until evening without eating after the Isrealities were defeated by the men of Ai (Joshua 7: 6).

Brethren, when you remember that you're in distress, you have been walloped of shame, of fear. The time of defeat of shame, of fear is a fine time to pray with fasting.

Let all who are in trouble call upon God. If you find difficulty in getting an answer from Heaven, then fast and pray, sincerely laying everything aside, as far as necessary, to seek God's face and find his will and blessing.

2. What displeases God in our life? Many Christians who do not prosper could learn the reason; if he would wait before God in such sincerity and abandon of self that he would not eat, would not sleep or would not carry on the regular affairs of life until God revealed what wrong in their life.

3. Genuine repentance. Unless we deliberately take time for meditation and examination of our hearts and waiting on God, we have no real sense of sin, no genuine horror at our guilt. I know that in under to be saved, one may turn immediately to Christ, as soon as he knows himself a sinner and knows Christ died for him. Oftentimes, our pretends turning to God is insincere and shallow, with no real sorrow for sin, no effort at restitution, no genuine change in attitude of heart. The ghastly wickedness of sin is hidden from us light hearted modern. Surely, often it would please God, if we would take time apart to search our hearts and find what pleases God and wholly forsake as far as we can consciously do so, in our sins. If we spend enough time in prayer and fasting this will help us to break up fallow ground of our hearts.

4. It leads us to victory over sin. Many Christians who have trusted God, who sincerely love him, who are going to Heaven and other Christians who say they cannot control their tempers, they have trouble in surrendering even enough to give God regularly the tithe. Christians find it hard to forgive one another and are constantly falling under the temptation. Is there victory for such Christians? Yes, there is but only found in the fasting and prayer. Every Christians. I think, should occasionally fast and pray waiting before God until he gets the victory that he needs. If you do not have victory over sin, then wait before God, pay whatever price that is necessary to secure his favor and the assurance of his help.

CHAPTER THIRTEEN

BIG PRAYERS, BIG ANSWERS FROM GOD

God delights to answer prayers for big things because he is not only the infinite and almighty God but the loving Father of his children. If the creation of the world proves God's power, then the giving of his own son in redeeming love save lost men proves his willingness to bless. " I am the Lord thy God which brought thee out of the Land of Egypt, open thy mouth wide and I will fill it" (Ps 81:10). God is able to answer any kind of prayer, answers them to any extent, provided only that, to answer the prayers would be right, God cannot lie, cannot sin, cannot be tempted. God in his infinite power authority do anything that is right. God has power to give mighty answer to prayer but he has the disposition. God is able and willing to answer big prayers for mighty things.

In Isaiah 59:1, says "Behold, the Lord's hand is not shortened, that it cannot save, either his ear heavy that it cannot hear". His hand reaches out as far as ever in power and his ear listens as willingly as ever in his kindness towards men. How little our unbelieving hearts know about God's willingness to answer prayers wonderfully, mighty to his own glory? "Call unto me and I will answer thee and show thee GREAT AND MIGHTY THINGS, which thou know not" (Jer 33:3) God has so much to give and we are so needy. And he would be gloried before men at an opportunity to answer big prayers. Yet our unbelieving hearts ask so little. I think of every one of us it must be said, as it was Nazareth. "He did not do, many mighty works there because of their unbelief" (Math 13:58) We ought to ask big things from God, many sins are mentioned in connection with prayer. People are warned not to pray to be seen of men and not to ask for something to consume it upon their own lusts. We are warned of how unforgivenness, covetousness, disobedience, unbelief and wrong home life hinder prayer. But of all the sins mentioned regarding prayer, not once does the scripture hint that any man ever asked too much from God.

Once of our greatest sins is that we do not ask for enough. We do not take what God is willing to give. We do not give God an opportunity to prove his love and power. God forgive us our little, stingy, unbelieving prayers.

GOD COMMANDS US TO ASK BIG THINGS

In the bible God has given us promises that he is willing to answer prayers for mighty things. He is pleading with us, to argue with us, to urge us to give him a chance to answer prayers for big things. The scripture gives a plain command about this and disobedience to us, it lead to sin. Here I give some scriptures. Let them transform your praying and faith routine. " I am the Lord thy God which brought thee out of the Land of Egypt, open thy mouth wide and I will fill it. (Ps 81:10). Here, God gives his credentials and offers proof of his ability and resources to accomplish big things. "Do you need a really big God to do something for you"? Then call on me, for I am the Lord thy God which brought thee out of Land of Egypt. I opened the red sea in answer to Moses payer. I brought all the plagues upon Egypt and others and then I brought my people out between the piled up waters of the red sea. I showed my mighty power by wondrous miracles as they journeyed. Then I caused the people to cross the flooded Jordan on ground while the waters and the wall of Jericho to fall down flat. That is the kind of God I am talking about brethren.

If you want your big thing done, you can call upon him, his is able to do it. He still can do mighty works, if you will believe in him.

God seems to be so jealous about his own great name and he constantly reminds us that he never changes. " I am the Lord, I changes not" (Malachi 3: 6). "Jesus the same yesterday and today and forever" (Heb 13: 8).

The scripture says "Ye have little, because ye ask little" (James 4: 2) Ask big you will get bigger bites from God. God wants his people-Children to open their mouths wide to receive the mighty blessings he is so able and willing to bestow. "Call unto me and I will answer thee and show thee great and mighty things which thou known not" (Jer 33:3). God here expects us to call on him and he will give "Great and mighty things which thou know not". God have in mind big prayers, asking great things are our right from God.

See from the scriptures the hunger of God's heart for somebody who will believe on him. Somebody who will give God chance to do great and mighty things in his life, "Is there anything too hard for me "? How anxious God is to prove his mighty power, he only waits until we ask him for great and mighty things. Can God give these great and mighty things? "Which thou knows not. God has greater things to give us, if we call upon him for mighty things and give him a chance and believe. God says, " If ye have faith as grain of mustard seed, ye shall say unto this mountain remove hence to yonder place and it shall remove and nothing shall be impossible unto you" (Math17:20).

Nothing is impossible to those who pray with faith. Because of our unbelief, we cannot ask mountain to remove into the sea, but assurance is that we were given right to pray, for big things. Jesus said all things are possible to him that believed (Math 9:23). Here our savior challenges us to ask for bigger things. Jesus added his wonderful statement that "What things so-ever ye desire, when ye pray," we can have it, if we believe that we receive them. And also our savior is telling us that starting and wonderful miracles can be done in answer to the prayer of faith. We should ask for mighty things and believe in God.

God is able to do exceeding abundantly above all, that we ask or think. This wonderful promise shown that God intended the marvelous answers to prayer to continue through all ages, having wonders done by the Holy Spirit who worked in us and these wonders should be done in the name of Jesus Christ, glorifying God.

Finally, the next time you pray, remember you are promised that you have an exceeding abundantly able God who can give more than you can even think or ask.

PRAYERS THAT DEMANDS GREAT THINGS FROM GOD.

There is no history throughout the bible where any man expected too much from God's hand or that it displeased God because we asked for mighty things.

Brethren, if God does not at first answer you prayer on big things or any discouraging circumstances seem to indicate that he will not hear you, do not be discouraged. If you know that what you are asking will honor God, then demand it, again and again and expect the answer.

Another illustration of how eager God is to give more than we can ask and how pleased he is with the big prayer is how Elisha, the man who demanded and received double portion of the Holy Spirit that rested on Elijah.

Time and space would fail us to call your attention other such marvelous prayers, marvelous answers in the bible. But for the strengthening of your faith in a mighty God who delights to opened the earth and swallowed up wicked men who challenged his leadership. (Num 16:25-35).

In reviewing these scriptures, any heart must see that God intended us to be encouraged to pray great prayers.

I will suggest, it would be blessed exercise to expend some days in carefully re-reading all the great answers to prayer which you can find in the bible and mediating upon the mighty promises of God.

ARE THERE BLESSINGS ON BIG PRAYERS?

Sometimes small prayers are the sign of weak faith and little faith grieves God and does great harm. Big prayers show faith in God. This pleases God and brings other blessed results. The God's people live in poverty in sickness, in disappointment and defeat because they do not pray for big things.

In conclusion, we have a great God. There is nothing too hard for our God. He loves us, he wants us to have all our need met. Will you today brethren, take his blessed promises and begin to pray the kind of prayers that he will allow God to do the wonderful things he want to do for us?

CHAPTER FOURTEEN

DOES GOD WORK MIRACLE TODAY? "YES"

He works today through miracles and to answers to prayers. "If thou canst believe, all things are possible to him that believeth" (Mark 9.23). Answer to prayer is one of the miracles. There must be a personal God who bears an individual cry and so, order events that the one who prayed gets what he would not get through natural means.

Answer to prayer means that God supernaturally intervenes and gives what would not be given without this miraculous intervention. "Why should it be thought a thing in credible with you that God should raise the death?" (Acts 26:8) The question asked today is does God works miracles?.

In reply to this question, whether God works miracles today unbelief. The question deserves an honest investigation in the light of God's word and in the facts of word wherever found.

GOD PROMISES MIRACLES IN ANSWER TO PRAYERS

Anyone who trusts in bible must see that Jesus promised miracles to those who believe in him when they prayed. Let us consider these promises "If ye have faith as a grain of mustard seed ye shall say unto this mountain remove hence to yonder place and it shall remove and nothing shall be impossible unto" (Math 17: 20). The savior generalizes his teaching in these strong words "And nothing shall be impossible unto you"? For those who have faith nothing is impossible. For they have at their command the miracles- Working power of God. Jesus promises the disciples that they can do the same kind of physical miracles, if they have faith and do not doubt. They can cause a fig tree or remove mountain and cast it into the sea if they have faith. Jesus promises. "And all things, whatsoever ye shall ask in prayer, believing, ye shall receive". The scripture does not mean that all who trust in Christ for salvation get miracles, but it certainly does mean that in any particular matter one who believes will find the thing possible that he has faith for.

We must remember that faith is a gift of God and the Holy Spirit will not help us to have faith about wicked things out of the will of God. The point is quite plain here that a miracle was possible in the apostles' days in answer to the prayer of faith and that anything else in the world in any day can have a miracle on exactly the same conditions when we adopts fasting and prayer.

And then, Jesus gave the general law of miracles in answer to prayer when he concludes in (Mark11.24). "Therefore I say unto you, what things so-ever ye desire, when ye pray, believe that ye receive them and ye shall have them". It is a blessing to remember here specifically that miracle is an object of conversation and things he has in mind when he gave this blessed promise.

Anybody who has enough faith in Christ can do his work, that same kind of work that Jesus had been doing. Certainly, then the savior promised miracles to those who as things purely in his name. That is when one can ask a thing wholly in Jesus' name or with his authority and for his sake, with his approval, then one can get it even, if it be a miracle.

Jesus gave great commission in (Mark 16:15-18). "Go ye into the entire world and preach the gospel to every creature. He that believeth and is baptized shall be saved, but he that believeth not shall be damned. And those signs shall follow then that believe, in my name shall they cast out devils, they shall speak with new tongues, they shall take up serpents and if they drink any deadly thing, it shall not hurt them, they shall lay hands on the sick and they shall recover"

This means that the promise shall follow every saved person. It is only a promise to people who have faith for these signs. One who trusts Christ for salvation gets salvation. One who has faith to cast out devils would cast out devils and who had faith to speak in a language that was new to him, would get power to do it exactly as the disciples did at Pentecost.

I think, it is important to remind you that the Lord Jesus never mean the miraculous signs to be the play thing of the curious. These signs were never to exalt men. No one in bible times ever picked up a snake and let it bite him to show his faith. No one in bible times drank poison to show that it would not harm him.

We may be sure that God signally honored with supernatural manifestation the work of other of his servants everywhere they went, that is, as often as it could honor his name and as often as they had faith for it. Miracles were never done to just to show off, never came just at anybody's whim, but were always the answer to somebody's faith for that particular instance. Christianity is miracle religion. Christianity teaches that a man must be supernaturally, miraculously born again by direct act of God the Holy Spirit, making him a new creature. The scripture teaches clearly that God directly, supernaturally answers prayer that the Holy Spirit of God literally dwells in the bodies of saved people, to direct them to comfort them, to give them wisdom and power in a wholly supernatural manner.

In (Colossian 1:16.17) says "For by him were all things created, that are in heaven and that are in earth, visible and invisible, whether they are in thrones or dominions or principalities or powers and things were created by him and for him and he is before a thing and by him all things consist".

You will notice that life itself in every day is surrounded with invisible miracles, if we believe, if we are conscious that the Holy Spirit of God lives within us, that angels are all about us, that a miracles- working God still sustains all things, it will be easier for us to believe that God can and will answer our prayers, that he has limitless ability and willingness to do what we need do for us whom he loves so well.

IS THE DAYS OF MIRACLES GONE?

When miracles are past, it is because the faith of God's people has worn. If the gift of prophecy is the normal thing for testament churches then that means that the miracles, supernatural working of God is to continue down through the ages in his church. The Christians believe that God's miracles concerning the bible did not end when John wrote the last words of the book of revelation. The bible itself is a living miracle. "The word of God is quick and powerful" (Heb 4:12). So, we should be careful and not go to either of two extreme, let us not insists that the working of the Holy Spirit of God in manifesting his power by miracles and signs is past and on the other hand, let us not say that he will always so act, if we ask him to do so. The measure in which he delights to work is left with him to continue. So God still works miracles in answer to prayer.

Brethren, we should seek of God presence in our life always to see the goodness what God has been doing in our life daily. Daniel survived several attempts on his life and his friends because of their open faith, he had on the God. He was thrown into the den of lions and with his three friends were tossed alive into a fiery furnace. Each occasion God proved himself, gave miraculous deliverance. The secret of Daniel's was that he prayed his way out to life. The result was that God was with him. And (Daniel 9.3) says "And I set my face unto the Lord God, to seek by prayer and supplications with fasting and sackcloth and ashes". The angel explained to the prophet that from the first day that he set himself to get an answer from God, his words had been heard and that the angel had been sent to him. So, brothers and sisters God had heard your fasting and prayer today when you do, in Jesus name.

CHAPTER FIFTEEN

PRAYER HINDRANCES

This chapter is a test of our faith in the Lord, concerning our blessing from God, through prayer.

If we pray without receiving God promises concerning our situation, is like God does not exist. In (1 peter 5:12) says "For the eyes of the Lord are over the righteous and his ears are open unto their prayers, but the face of the Lord is against them that do evils". One of the things that can hinder our prayer not to be heard is when we are in sin.

We do lot of evils against God, against fellow human beings and our prayer remains abomination to God and he will not answer our prayer. The psalmist said in (psalm 66:18), "If I regard iniquity in my heart, the Lord will not hear me".

The normal Christian life is a life of regular, daily answer in prayer. Following the model prayer taught by Jesus to his disciples, state that we should pray daily for bread and expect to get it and to ask daily for forgiveness, for deliverance from the evil once and other needs and daily to get the answers they sought. We shouldn't be having difficulties in our prayer, if will all follow the teaching of the Lord Jesus about prayer shows that we too have a normal day to day in hindered relationship with God. The promises of asking and receiving, seeking and finding, knocking and having God open to us, has never fed. God clearly said "Until now, you have not asked for anything in my name. Ask and you will receive and your joy will be complete" (John 16:24). It is proper to infer that God intended asking to be followed by having and that the Christian in the will of God can live day to day in the fullness of joy of having his prayers answered. It is perfectly normal for an obedient child to ask for bread every meal and get it, get all he wants and eat until he is perfectly satisfied. When a Christian fails to have his prayer, he should regards it as sign that something is wrong that needs attention at once. When I set in the morning to go to work, I start my vehicle it doesn't start, I know that something is wrong and I would immediately set out to find out what was wrong.

So, also every Christian ought to be in daily communion with God and ought to live the joy full of life answered prayer. And when anything hinders his prayers, the Christian ought immediately to be able to find out what is wrong and get it corrected.

SINS THAT HINDER PRAYERS

There are sins that hinder the prayer of Christians, sins that turn God's face totally away so that he will not hear, sins which makes it so possible that God cannot, in righteousness, heed the cry of his own child whom he loves. We are not left alone in the dark about these sins, God in his infinite love, has shown us in the scripture the things that grieve him, the things that makes it so impossible he cannot fully answer our prayer.

Sometimes, we pray for daily bread or for daily necessities such as money for accommodation, for job, for cloths or furniture, things for which God tells us to pray and yet no answer comes, Christians often pray for the conversion of loved ones, pray for revivals, pray for help in temptation, all matters about which God has declared in his word that he is concerned and which he is anxious to give us, yet Christian often do not get the answer to their payers. Why?. This is because our prayer cannot be answered by a Holy God because of our sins in the life and heart of the one who prays.

It may be that you have some of your prayers answered that does not mean that our Dear Lord has answered you. Remember that he "Sendest rain on the just and unjust" (Matt 5:45). God may give you many things that do not come because he respects your prayers and answered them, but because of his infinite mercy which is poured out even upon the worst sinners.

God who still gives breath to the murderer, food to the man who never prays, the God who gives all the bounties of nature to a sinning, that God still loves and cares for his children even when they live in sin and grieve his heart. May be, what God has been doing for you when you prayed was not at all the answer to your prayers but just such mercies as his infinite love and goodness provide the wicked of his creatures.

Whether God hears some of your prayers or not, none of them, I mean your prayers hindered, if you do not day by day live in the fullness of answered prayer. Due to sins in our life, we are painfully, conscious that our prayers are not heard. How important it is to clear that live between you and God, so he will hear you, how important it is to confess and forsake everything that grieves the Dear Holy Spirit and shuts up heaven to your prayers and stops God's ears.

Let us brethren, prayerfully examine the world of God and search our heart to see why our prayers hindered and why God does not answer to give us what we ask.

BAD RELATIONSHIP HINDERS PRAYER (ESPECIAL HUSBAND AND WIFE).

Wife: The prayer of wife can be hindered, if she is not submissive to his husband. God spoke about the sins of rebellious wife that hurts her prayers. God speaks to the wife about her duty to the husband. (1 Tim 2:11-13).

And in the matter of getting your prayers answered, it does not matter says the Lord, what kind of husband you have, you must obey him, you must be subject to his authority. A woman must be subject to her husband or her prayers be hindered. He went further to explained that the man may even be an unsaved Christian, one who will not obey the word of God, who will not listen to the bible, who will not attend church services, yet a Christian woman is to be subject to such to such a husband, so that her prayers will not be hindered.

The wife's prayer for the salvation of her husband may be blocked by her own disobedience. A woman may seek to use her influence with the husband by adoring her body by the plaiting of her hair, by the weaving of gold or by her neat and attractive dress but the Lord God here says that these things are not to be the beauty, the adornment, the attraction of a Christian woman and they will not win her husband, they will not get her prayers answered, But every woman is to have " Ornament" of a meek and quiet Spirit, which is in the sight of God of great price.

Women, it is not wrong to plait your hair or wear cloths but the only ornament to win a husband for God is the ornament that will cause God to answer your prayers, the ornament of meek and obedient Spirit. Example in the bible was Sarah, the wife of Abraham, she even called her husband- Abraham "Lord" and she obey her husband. Christian women, if your prayers are not to be hindered, you must be subject to your husbands.

How earnestly a woman prayed, how diligently she attended the house of God, how eagerly she did church work and God seemed not to hear her prayers about an unsaved husband or son or daughter. It is also remarkable fact that in nearly every congregation of Christians, Godly women, who pray, who read their bibles, who live lives mere or less separated from worldliness in general, yet who cannot get their prayers answered. The answer is not found in the public church services. If you watch such good women singing in the choir, teaching Sabbath school lessons, attending bible conferences, giving money to the poor, you wonder why are their prayers not answered?. The sins that hindered our prayers are primarily home-sins.

Dear wife, you need this, if you are guilty of this horrible home sin of rebellion against the one whom you took with solemn vows as yor husband, to honor, love and obey, then that sin today hinders your prayers. That rebellion is the Secret of why God has turned away his face and many of your prayers go unanswered.

Beloved, Christian wife, remember your husbands are the authorities of the homes. Therefore, a rebellion against authority is the heart of all crime and every criminal in a prison has first be guilty neither of murder, nor of thief but of rebellion against constituted authority. God says that if you will not be subjected to your husband, your prayers are to be hindered.

HUSBAND YOUR REQUIREMENTS AT HOME.

1. Husbands, you are to dwell with your wives. "According to knowledge" that is based on an understanding of the scripture relating to husband and wife.
2. "Giving honor unto the wife, as unto the weaker vessel".
3. "As being heirs together of the grace of life".

Husband should take the place accorded to him in the bible as the head of the home, high priest unto God, responsible for the home and for the children. " The husband is the head of the wife even as Christ is the head of the church" (Eph 5: 23).

A husband who does not dwell with the wife according to knowledge of the plan commanded by scripture is likely to have the prayers unanswered-hindered his prayers.

THE DUTIES OF HUSBANDS.

Dear Christian husband, remember that you are stronger than your wife.

1. You should be an exemplary to your wife.
2. You should be able to explain the scripture to your wife (1 Corith 14: 35).

3. You have heavy responsibilities of earning your family living.
4. Disciplining the children at home.
5. Taking the family to Christ.
6. Giving religions instruction in the home and that of family and alike.

A husband who shirks and avoids these responsibilities,

Leaving them for her weaker partner is sin before God and will have his prayers hindered. And husband should feel himself as one with his wife as one flesh. "No man ever hated his own flesh but nornisheth and cherisheth it". (Eph 5:29). Husband love your wife as Christ loved the church and gave his life for it.

WARNING TO HUSBANDS

Husband the total surrender to God's pattern for the place in the home is essential to form the happy life of daily answered prayer. The slack husband will find that his prayers are hindered.

Disagreement in the home grieves God. And Children who rebel against their parents, let them know that such rebellion turns away the face of God and stops his ears and hinders their prayers.

Husband and wife should submit themselves to the will of God and obedience to his plan in the home is more important than any kind of public worship, than any duty. The hindrance to prayer when you fasted is often in the relation of wives and husbands and of children parents in the home. Your home front determines your peace, happiness, progress and relationship with outside people that is your future, lays the peace at home Christians. Praise God.

We believe, if a wife's prayers are hindered by the sin of rebellion against husband and the husband's prayers are hindered by not taking his scriptural position in the home and relation to his wife, it is also true that every wrong against others which is not made right stands between the Christian and God to hinder our prayers.

OTHER HINDRANCES OF PRAYERS

DEBTS UNPAID: Debts own to your fellow being not paid constitute hindrance to your prayers. How could God be pleased to bless his own children who have not then honestly turned away from sin in their own lives?.

Businessmen are crying out, sometimes fellow church members cried out, if the members of our church would pay us what they owes us either in form of loan borrowed or sales products or business transaction between member, they would feel pleased more like going to church.

Anyone who is well acquainted with retail credit business will knows that multitudes of church people will not pay honest debts unless the owners follows them up to get it. Sometimes Christians move out of apartments or houses owing backlogs of rent which they never pay. Sometimes Christians owes long standing debts to Doctors who cared for them in the time of deepest distress of their life without paying. Brother borrows money from Christian Brother, promising heaven and earth to repay it within a certain time, then debt becomes so old that he is ashamed to pay it and resulted not attending to church services.

Dear brethren reader of this book, I beg you in the name of our Lord Jesus, if you have debt(s) unpaid in your life or of recent when you pray you remember it, go now and pay it, so that God will hear your prayers.

Remember beloved, that you are God's own child, as dear as the apple of his eyes, you may be as dear to him as was David, a man after his own heart or a Samson, a judge of Israel or a Peter, the first apostle but I solemnly warn that God hates sin, even in the dearest of his children or honor his word more than his honor his name. God demands that you forsake it that you hates sin that you honestly try to make right thing you have done wrong.

UNRECONCILED BROTHERS HINDER PRAYERS

Unreconciled with offended brother brings reproach in our LIFE. "If bring thy gift to the altar and there remembered that thy brother hath hurt against thee, leave there thy gift before the altar and go thy, first to reconciled, so thy brother and then come and offer thy gift" (Matt 5: 23, 24).

The Lord Jesus clearly said that, if one should bring a Lamb for a sacrifice or any kind of an offering to God and there at the altar should remember a brother whom he had wronged or offended, then he must at once stop the sacrifice "Leave that Lamb with its tied together on the ground before the altar, until you go and make right the wrong done your brother. If not, nothing you can do for me, can be viewed with favor, said the savior. Some of us pray long and God never hears us. Some of us give much money and the sight of God it is an abomination to God. Some of us work and toil doing "Church work" and God hates our prayers.

Anything you offer to God is hateful in his sight, if you will not go and reconciled to your brother and others you have offended.

Many of us cannot get our prayers heard because already the cry of others whom we have offended has been heard by God, example is Cain-Cain tried to talk to God but the blood of his slain brother, Abel had cried out of the ground to God against Cain. And the Lord warns in (Exodus 22: 22, 23). "Any afflicted widow or fatherless child could cry would be heard and God's wrath would wax hot against those who oppressed them".

You had as well never offer them any more thing, until you make a genuine efforts to pay the bills you own to right the wrongs you have done, to apologize for sins committed and to be reconciled with others.

HINDRANCES IN UNFORGIVENESS GRIEVES GOD.

Beloved brethren, do you know that unforgiveness grieves God?. Unforgiveness blocks the daily prayers, cleansing and forgiveness and so hinders our prayers. Unforgiveness, holding grudges or enmity against others, may seen to be a very respectable sin in us. People who would not steal, who will never get drunk, who will not gamble, who will never scorn lie are yet guilty of this wicked sin.

Our Lord savior plainly said in Matthew "So likewise shall my heavenly do also unto you, if ye from your hearts forgive not everyone, his brother their trespasses". Peter asked Jesus Christ, how many times shall we forgive one who sins against us? Jesus answered "I say unto thee, until seventy times seven, but until seventy times seven times seven". And when you have forgiven the same person 490 times, no doubt you will have lost count. Terrible punishment will be the lot of every Christian who carries a grudge and unforgiveness in his heart.

Note: Dear brethren, the savior said this forgiveness must be from your hearts. To live normally at peace is not enough. Sometimes a Christian will say. "Well, I will forgive her but I will never forget" or a brother may say "I will forgive him because it has been commanded to me in the scripture but I will never have anything more to do with him". Such forgiveness is not forgiveness at all in God's sight. When God forgives, he forgets. How would you like for God to say about your own case. "Well, I will forgive your sins, but I never want to have anything more to do with you"?. That is not a genuine forgiveness.

In God's grace, a Christian can so forgive that every memory brings not bitterness but a sweet sense of peace without any rancor or bitterness whatever.

If we want to be like Jesus, we must forgive. Dying on the cross, he prayed about the people who crucified him, who mocked him while he died, who gave him vinegar mingled with gall, when he was thirsty, who had spit in his face and these he prayed for. "Father forgive them for they know not what they do".

Finally, Dear Christian, Our Lord's prayer is to be a daily prayer for daily bread and daily needs and confessing daily sins. And that indicates that every Christian, every day ought to go about this important matter of seeing that all the grudges are forgiven.

Thus "let not the sun go down upon your wrath". A grudge, if left in the heart overnight may so take root as to embitter your whole life and ruin the testimony. Before sun down every day search out your heart, judge every little grudge, every bit of enmity, every slightest passion of unforgiveness. Confess it to God as a sin and turn your heart away from it and God will take it away and cleanse it. Know that, if you do not forgive neither will you be forgiven.

CHAPTER SIXTEEN

LACK OF PRAYER IS A SIN.

Prayerlessness is another name of unbelief. A child of God, prayerlessness is identify with backsliding. Prayerlessness is the father and partner of every vile sin, the father of drunkenness and lust is the father of adultery. It has been identified that prayerlessness itself is worse than murder, worse than adultery, worse than blasphemy. It is more fundamental and more clearly reveals to hear. The fact remains while murder, adultery and blasphemy may catch a person unaware, trapped by the carnal mind, prayerlessness is the very heart of the carnal mind itself states of alienation from God.

Your greatest sin and mine too, is prayerlessness. My indecision, my lack wisdom, my lack of guidance comes directly out of my prayerlessness. All the times, I have fallen into sin, I have failed in my duties, I have been bereft of power or disconsolate for lack of comfort, I can charge it to the sin of prayerlessness. It is a sin when we pray without faith. It is sad beyond expression when wrong home life, when wrongs unrighted, when unforgiveness or rebellion or distaste for the bible or any secret love of sin hindered our prayers.

The greatest sin at all is not to pray. Our greatest problem is not that we pray wrongly but we pray little or do not pray at all. Prayer should be definite, direct, determinedly going to God to get things, is an unknown and inexperienced process to most Christians. This prayerlessness is back of all the fruitlessness, powerlessness and joylessness in the average Christian life. The scripture recorded that prayerlessness is a sin, (Samuel 12: 23) when Samuel told the people of Israel, "God forbids that I should sin against the Lord in ceasing to pray for you". In (1thess 5: 17), we were told to pray all the time. "Pray without ceasing", men ought always to pray and never give up, that is the commanded of Jesus Christ, not to obey and it is a sin. The Christian is commanded to put on the whole armor of God, the girdle of truth, the breast plate of righteousness, the shoes of the Gospel of peace, the shield of faith, the helmet of salvation, the sword of the spirit. "By praying always with all prayer and supplication in the spirit and watching their, unto with all perseverance and supplication for all saints" (Eph 6: 18).

Jesus warns his disciples more than one to watch and pray lest they enter into temptation. When we refuse to pray, we are rebels, disobedient. Prayer ought to arise from the heart like the fragrance from burning incense on an altar. The soul of a Christian can be so possessed of God, so hungry for his presence, which both the conscious and the subconscious mind carry on the pleading, the searching for God's face and his will and way and work. How great is our sin when we do not pray?.

Prayerlessness is a sin because it leaves the door open for all other sins to come in. In fact, prayer is the remedy for temptation. Prayer is the way to defeat the evil one. By prayer one may be able to stand against the viles of devil and to withstand in the evil day. A word of meditation which says "Satan tremble when he sees the weakest saint on his knees". If that saint sin really, directly and persistently calls for God for God to help him against sin and to keep him out of temptation and to defeat the evil one. "Prayer will make a man cease from sin, as sin will entice a man to cease from praying".

Many do not have daily necessities because they do not pray as they are commanded to pray. No doubt many of the afflicted are still afflicted because they have not obeyed God's command. "Is any among you afflicted? Let him pray". And many of the sick remain sick because they do not "Call for the elders of the church and let them pray over him, anointing him with oil in the name of the Lord, as the Lord said and so have not received the blessing promised that "The prayer of faith shall save the sick and if he has committed sins, they shall be forgiven him". (James 5:13, 15).

"If any of you lack wisdom, let him ask of God that giveth to all men liberally and up braideth not" (James 1: 5). They do not ask and therefore do not receive. They do not seek and therefore they do not find. They do not knock, and therefore the door is not opened (Matt 7: 7, 8).

Many of God's children go through this world as an orphan as if God did not love them, as if God were not able or willing to care for his own. Many Christians die prematurely because they do not pray. The scripture do not teach that one who prays may live forever, without dying but it certainly does teach that many die prematurely when they might live longer with great blessing if they had prayed. And so, because of our prayerlessness we miss many, many blessing, people are sick when they might be well, some die when they might have live. Businesses fail when they might have prosper. And people go hungry and without proper clothing who might have be covered and fed to the glory of God, if they would have prayed.

Another thing "God plainly promise to hear from his people when they come in humility and with prayer and with prayer and supplication and repentance heart" (2 chron 7: 14). The result of prayerlessness is that God's work suffers and languishes, if people would but pray, pray earnestly, pray effectively, pray with a Holy abandon God's work would not languish. The decay in the churches, the cooling of revival fires and the lukewarmness in the churches are the fruit of our prayerlessness. If we work harder and the body needs more food, we hanger for it and when eat more, if you enjoyed praying more than other things you do, you would do more praying.

PRAYERLESSNESS PROVES THAT WE DO NOT REALLY ENJOY GOD

Brethren, let us be honest in searching our own heart here. Do we not often pray simply as a matter of duty?. If we are born-again children of

God, then we love him. In our hearts we have received the Holy Spirit of adoption whereby we cry "Abba Father". Many of us do not really enjoy our heavenly Father and we spend little time in his company or presence, little time asking for his blessings and receiving those he has offered.

How can we pray, if we do not believe it pays? How can we pray, if we do not believe we get anywhere or get something from God? When we are sick we go to the doctor first instead of praying. Is it not obviously that one who believes that will pray before he does other things?.

I think there is no doubt that our prayerlessness proves that we have little confidence in getting answers to our prayers.

I know many people who do say "I believe in prayer as much as any other person or I have lots of faith in God, yet when they were sick they depended on doctors and when they were out of job they depended on employment agencies and need, they were in need they called relatives for help before calling on God. The living faith, absolutely must express itself in calling on God for what we need and desire. Prayerlessness proves our laziness. Prayer is hard work. It demands though, concentration and persistence. One who becomes great in prayer must have overcome every kind handicaps, discouragement and temptation. "A successful Christian is a prayable Christian" Satan would keep us from prayer by make us too busy at other matters, or weak. Many have learned the agonies in prayer, to labor as Jacob wrestled with the angel at penile (Gen. 32: 24-31). Jacob wrestled with angel of God in dream, also do Rachel, the barren wife, prayed without ceasing that she might not be outdone by her mocking sisters and of her prayer, she said "With great wrestling's have I wrestled with my sisters and I have prevailed". The fact proves that we do not pray, meaning we are lazy, indifferent Christians with little heart for the work of God. We read newspapers, watch films, play with computers, internets, videos, dvd's instead of praying because we are more interested in these things we watch and read, talk about them. We are interested in these things instead of what we would have talk to God. We spend more time discussing with other people than we do in talking to God, we really think more of other people than we do to God.

We Christian workers may even spend more time in our sermons, our libraries, our visiting friends, our church programmes because we are more about these incidents and secondary matters than we do about the main matters. Does it not mean that our love, our interest, our desire is on other things first? And the little that we pray proves how little we are interested in God's will for us and in bringing souls to Christ and advancing the work that is truly his . Some will be tempted to say that they have so much work to do, good work indeed, honorable, necessary work, that they cannot pray as much as my teaching here. That is impossible for the greatest men of God, the busiest, found time for that kind of praying.

Even Jesus Christ spends long seasons in prayer. He went up to mountain to pray. He prayed all night in the wilderness. Sometimes men of God must get to bed late ad often they are late risers, speaking in the evening and finding it hard to relax and sleep immediately after the greatest labor and excitement of the day, evangelist and preachers best rest after midnight. It is remarkable fact that the men who have been the most abundant in labors for God have the ones who spent the greatest amount of time prayer.

Our excuses are that the, we do not pray more because we do not think prayer is as important as the other things we do. We think also visiting is more important than prayer and we think sleep is more important than in prayer.

HOW TO OVERCOME PRAYERLESSNESS

1. We suggest, we set apart a season of time early in every day to pray, along with meditation in the bible. That is put prayers first by having a season of prayers before anything else of importance in the day. You probably will have to rise earlier than you now rise. You may have to leave off other matters of lesser importance. God says in (proverbs 8: 17). "Those that seek me early shall find me".

2. Make it a habit of praying through every burden and problem that come to you. We may not in one day get the full answer to our great prayer, but we can every day believe and get a sweet peace to know that the thing in the hands of our Heavenly Father and he has smiled into our hearts and he has given us peace. You can pray until you have assurance that God has undertaken and will do the thing you desire or you can pray until God's Holy Spirit helps you see how you should modify your prayer to fit with the plan of God. That means leave every worry, every anxiety with Jesus every day.

3. Take time to pray about things as they come up. It will be impossible to remember all the requests for prayer that would come to you in a day's time. I ever promise to pray for any matter in the future excepts as God lays it on my heart and bring it to my mind. I have found a great peace in going to God with every burden the moment I feel the need for praying about it.

4. Leave all the formalities and let prayer be simply talking with God. Every Christians should stop and say, "Lord I did something wrong forgive me or Lord help me to know what to say to these men". Have a connecting prayer with every detail of your life with God. Leave off the forms of set prayers and get accustomed to talking to God as simply as a little child talks to his mother.

5. Follow the bible examples and teachings about prayers. Jacob prayed all nights, so did Jesus. Then I would enter into the fullness of prayer life by praying all night. I will never forget the fullness of blessing that came in some nights of prayer in the Galily. I think it is shameful that the great experiences of prayer in the bible are not duplicated in the lives of modern Christians.

In conclusion of fasting and prayer. Esther and her maidens fasted and prayed three days and nights. The people of Ninevah prayed without neither eating nor drinking for days until God heard and spared the city and saved them from distortion. The Apostles fasted and prayed for ten days.

Brethren, have you ever gone without meals or spent a day without food while you sought the food from Heaven? While your mind was absorbed in God and seeking his power alone? If the Pharisees cam entered into fasting as a form, a work of merit, why Christians can't fast and pray for burden for souls and to be filled with the power of God.

Taking the seriousness of fasting and prayer- Daniel went for three full weeks in which he ate no pleasant bread and ate no treat (Dan 10: 2-3). And should not, sometimes have times of mourning of confessing our sins of waiting on God in which we might for weeks eat only moderately doing only such work as we must until certain victories won, certain blessing obtained?. And from all these, let us learn the lesson that prayer with fasting is advance prayer.

Also let us get out of our ruts, let us pray when we are standing even when we are sitting for God to hear us.

In times of great emergency and distress we ought surely to be on our very faces before God, pleading and waiting on him. In other times, we should be like David to awake in the night, communing with our hearts upon our beds (Ps 4: 4).

Finally, Pray at morning, at noon, at evening (Ps 35: 17), Let us seek to enter into all the wealth of prayer especially. Let us immolate the bible characters as much as they prayed. Let us weep as much as they wept. Let us fast as much as they fasted.

Lastly let us make prayer the biggest, worship of our lives and greatest enjoyment and unceasing activity in our life.

CHAPTER SEVENTEEN

THE BELEIVERS' WEAPONS

Here we identify the weapons Christians could use over their enemies day after day. The under-listed are the believers' weapons against any enemy in our lives.

Satan understands and recognizes these names faster than any other names especially when you are communing with your God or a situation when you have emergencies in your life.

1. The name of Jesus:- This unseat any type of enemy, any obstacle, any impossibilities, any stubborn problems or any difficulties in our life.
2. The blood of Jesus:- This apply to the first, it neutralizes every forces of darkness, anywhere and in any situation operating.
3. The word of God:- The use of word of God in your prayer and meditation disorganizes any evil forces around you, either heavenly and earth and gives you the power to destroy the work of enemies.
4. The Christian Praises:- Almighty God always happy when you're praising him either day or night, no evil forces can break the atmosphere of praises.

Finally brethren, "Be strong in the Lord and in the power of his might, put on the whole armor of God that ye may be able to stand against the wiles of the devil". (Eph 6: 10, 11) "And they overcome him by the Blood of the Lamb and by the word of their testimony". (Rev 12: 11)

THE FOLLOWINGS ARE THE OPPRESSOR OF THE BELIEVERS. When you notice in your dream the followings listed below, wake-up and pray heavily against them.

- A dead relation visiting you.
- Marsquared pursing you.
- Mates swimming in the river.
- Mates bringing food and asking you to eat.
- A single having sexual intercourse.
- And others

If a Christian experienced the above in dream, you should not put it aside by the wave of the hand, but on getting out of sleep, you should examine your ways and confess any known sin unto God. Bind all those demons. Ask God to restore whatever had been tamptered in your life. You seek the help of God and council of matured Spiritual filled Christian head, older than you in faith.

"No weapons that is formed against thee shall prosper and every tongue that shall rise against thee in judgment thou shall condemn" (Isa 57:17).

The bible says "Behold they shall gather together, but not by me, whosoever shall gather together against thee shall fail for thy sake" (Isa 54:15). "When the enemy shall come in like a flood, the Spirit of God shall lift up a standard against him" (Isa 59: 19).

CONFESSIONS OF SINS

There are confessions and confessions stated in the word of God but the most significant ones are three as listed below.

1. Confessions of the Lordship of Christ. Accepting that Jesus Christ is Lord and savior, the maker of Heaven and Earth through him we shall be saved.
2. Confession of our faith in the word, in the Christ Jesus and in God the Father. Having your faith build in exclusively in our Lord Jesus.
3. Confession of our sins, identifying that we are sinners in the sight of God and seek for forgiveness of our sins always.

We should confess our affirmation to something we believe and testify to something that we know. Confession does not only mean confession of sin, it also involved witnessing of a truth that we have embraced in our life. "Our good God never intended that our circumstances should control his children, rather that the word of God in the mouth of the Christian should control it circumstances". I n Jer 23: 29) God is confirming his spoken word. "Is not my word like a fire, and like a hammer that brake the rock into pieces"?.

Christians should realize that when the name of Jesus is pronounced, what comes out of their mouth is fire. When a Christian stands on the authority given to him by Christ and give a command in Jesus' name, fire pours out of his mouth and any demon controlling the circumstance must obey. Jesus Christ is alive today to see to it that every word of his mouth comes to pass.

We shall remember the word of God is light unto them that believe in him. "Behold, I give unto you power (authority) to Thred upon serpents and over all the power of the enemy and Nothing Shall By Any Means Hurt You". (Luke 10: 19).

Beloved, persistent battling in prayer will in every case result in the ultimate route out of the enemy. God will, if necessary dispatch an Arch-Angel to the assistance of the man or woman who is faithful in prayer. We should realize that there is power in the name of Jesus. There is power in the blood of Jesus. The scripture says "And being found in fashion as a man, he humbled himself and become obedient unto death, even the death at the cross, wherefore God also had highly exalted, given Him a Name Which Is Above Every Other Name. That at name of Jesus every Knee shall bow, even things in Heaven and things on Earth and things under the Earth. Amen.

And that every tongue should confess that Jesus Christ is Lord, to the glory of God the Father. (Phil 2: 8-11). This is only weapon that keeps the enemy at bay. A Christian should not sleep over your own affairs, your life, your family, your business etc. There is no particular place where prayer cannot be said. Prayer could be offered anywhere, as enemies abound everywhere, in the house, at work, in the office, in the bus, in the Airline, in the plane, at sea, in safety, in danger etc.

Sometimes, we apply the fire bridge approach in our Christian lives, especially towards prayer. Most often, we wait until the devil knocks us down before we go down on our knees in prayer. We wait most times until we become ill, until our business begins to show signs of recession, until there is physical threat on our lives before we remember God.

QUOTABLE QUOTES FROM GOD'S PEOPLE

1. Persistence in prayer is the insurance against failure.
2. It is not how long you prayed, it is how nice or good, it is that matters.
3. Remember that prayers can't be answered until they are prayed (John C Maxwell).
4. Do deep praying before you find yourself in a deep hole (John I Mason)
5. The less I pray, the harder it gets, the more I pray the better it goes (Martin Luther).
6. Pray to do the will of God in every situation, nothing else is worth praying for. (John I Mason).
7. The devil smiles when we make plans. He laughs when we get too busy, he trembles when we pray (Carrie ten Boom).

HOW TO KNOW GOD

The steps of knowing God are listed below, read them and mediate with them always.

1. Recognize God loves you- Read John 3:16, John 17:3 and John 15: 9 etc.
2. Admit you need help- Read John 3:19, John 8: 24, John 3: 18
3. Believe that Jesus is the only savoir- Read John 1: 29, John 14: 6, John 3: 36.
4. Receive Jesus as your own savior- John 1: 12, John 10: 28, John 5: 24.
5. Acknowledge that Jesus is now your Lord and friend- John 15: 14, John 20: 28, John 16: 24.
6. Recognize now belong to God's family-Church Read John 20: 19-20, John 15: 6.
7. Commit yourself to serve the Lord. Pray and read the bible and witness for God. Read John 14: 13, John 8: 31-32, John 20:21.

Remain bless in Jesus' Name.